# Terry Johnson
# Plays: 2

## Imagine Drowning, Hysteria, Dead Funny

*Imagine Drowning*: 'An intriguing play; a mixture of fused-piece gothic mystery and moral homily . . . It keeps you on the edge of your seat and ambiguously combines mystery with morality.' *Guardian*

*Hysteria* produced at the Royal Court Classics season in 1995: 'Terry Johnson's excellent play encompasses so many genres that even Polonius might have trouble shackling them together: comical-farcical-tragical-historical-psychoanalytical just about covers it . . . the double or even treble levels on which the play operates is what makes it so enjoyable; there is stimulus along with the slapstick and, in the surrealist apotheosis . . . the most exciting gift the theatre can offer: sheer amazement.'
*The Times*
'Johnson has constructed a wondrous comedy of mistaken identity which darkens into a Freudian case history gone horribly awry.' *Spectator*
'Hysteria is that contemporary rarity, thoughtful and brilliantly developed farce which knows exactly when the laughter has to stop.' *Sunday Telegraph*

*Dead Funny*: 'Johnson has written another dazzlingly equivocal piece: one that questions the dubious sexual values of the great English drolls while invoking their hallowed memories and methods . . . He pushes the frontiers of farce into areas of real pain . . . an exhilarating play that is part custard-pie tragedy, part inquiring elegy for a vanishing music-hall tradition based on the principle that a dirty mind is a joy forever.' *Guardian*

**Terry Johnson**'s work as a playwright includes the version of Edward Ravenscroft's *The London Cuckolds*, recently produced at the Royal National Theatre; *Dead Funny* which opened at the Hampstead Theatre and enjoyed two successful West End runs at the Vaudeville and Savoy Theatres, and *Hysteria*, last seen at the Duke of York's theatre as part of the Royal Court Classics season. Also revived at the Donmar Warehouse was *Insignificance*. His earlier work includes *Amabel* and *Unsuitable for Adults* at the Bush, *Imagine Drowning* at Hampstead and *Cries from the Mammal House* at the Royal Court. His work has been performed all over Great Britain, in major US cities, Australia, Europe, Israel, Ireland and Canada. He is the recipient of some major British Theatre Awards including Playwright of the Year 1995; Critics' Circle Best New Play 1995; Writers' Guild Best West End Play 1995; Olivier Award Best Comedy 1994; the Mayer-Whitworth Award 1993 and the John Whiting Award 1991. He has directed new work at the Royal Court, Bristol Old Vic, Soho Poly and Hampstead Theatre. In 1996 he directed the American première of Stephen Jeffreys' *The Libertine* for Steppenwolf Theater in Chicago, and is currently directing at the Royal National Theatre. As a director for television he has just completed a film of *Neville's Island* by Tim Firth . . . . . . . . . . . . . . . . . . . . . . ter and *The Chemistry Lesson* to the BBC . . . . . . . . . . . . . . . . . . . . . . . des the adaptation of Alan Ayckbo

*by the same author*

Terry Johnson Plays: 1
(Insignificance, Unsuitable for Adults,
Cries from the Mammal House)

The London Cuckolds

# TERRY JOHNSON

# **Plays: 2**

Imagine Drowning
Hysteria
Dead Funny

*with an introduction by Nicholas Wright*

Methuen Drama

## METHUEN CONTEMPORARY DRAMATISTS

3 5 7 9 10 8 6 4 2

Published by Methuen 2003
Methuen Publishing Ltd
215 Vauxhall Bridge Rd
London SW1V 1EJ

*Imagine Drowning* copyright © 1991 by Terry Johnson
*Hysteria* first published by Methuen in the Royal Court Writers Series
in 1993, revised 1995, copyright © 1993, 1995, 1998 by Terry Johnson
*Dead Funny* first published 1994, revised 1998, copyright © 1994, 1998 by Terry Johnson.
Material on pages 257–259 copyright Sid Green and Dick Hills.
Material on page 260 copyright Jim Casey (the Estate of Jimmy James).
Short passage on page 271 copyright Ray Galton and Alan Simpson.
The author would like to thank Sid Green and Dick Hills; Jim Casey
(the Estate of Jimmy James); Ray Galton and Alan Simpson
for their kind permission to use original material in the play.

Introduction copyright © 1998 by Nicholas Wright

Terry Johnson has asserted his rights under the Copyright, Designs and
Patents Act, 1988 to be identified as the author of this work.

ISBN 0 413 72360 7

A CIP catalogue record for this book is available from the British Library

Typeset by Deltatype Ltd, Birkenhead, Merseyside
Printed and bound in Great Britain
by Cox & Wyman Ltd, Reading, Berkshire

# Contents

# Terry Johnson:
# A Chronology

1979    *Amabel* Bush Theatre

1981    *Days Here So Dark* Paine's Plough

1982    *Insignificance* Royal Court Theatre. SWET nominations for Best Play and Best Newcomer. Plays and Players Award, Evening Standard Award (Most Promising Playwright). Performed US, Germany, France, Australia, Israel, New Zealand, Japan.

1983    *Bellevue* Welfare State International

1984    *Cries from the Mammal House* Royal Court/Leicester Haymarket
*Unsuitable for Adults* Bush Theatre. Performed in US, New Zealand, Australia, Canada

1985    *Tuesday's Child* BBC TV. Co-written with Kate Lock
*Time Trouble* BBC TV
*Insignificance* Screenplay for Recorded Picture Co.

1986    *Tuesday's Child* Theatre Royal, Stratford East. Co-written with Kate Lock

1991    *Imagine Drowning* Hampstead Theatre. Winner of the John Whiting Award, 1991

1993    *Hysteria* Royal Court Theatre. Winner of the Olivier Award for Best Comedy 1993, and Writers' Guild Award for Best West End Play
*99 to 1* Carlton TV

1994    *Dead Funny* Hampstead, Vaudeville and Savoy Theatres. Winner of Critics' Circle Award for Best New Play, Writers' Guild Award for Best West End Play, 1994 Time Out Drama Award
*The Bite*, three-part television series for Warner Sister/Carlton Television

# Introduction

## 'Is man no more than this?'

Terry Johnson's first play *Amabel*, was produced in 1979, and he had his first great success with *Insignificance* three years later. This was an awkward moment for a playwright to appear, at least a male one. The radical writers of the early seventies had long since fallen off the perch, or flown to fame, fortune and the National Theatre. New playwrights were appearing in some quantity, but nearly all of them were women. So there wasn't a movement with which Johnson could be connected; he stood alone, an odd, unclassifiable voice, odd most of all in his demonstrable appeal to the public. Isolation of this kind has a muffling effect on a writer's career. People in the theatre and, (even more), people who write about the theatre, like their playwrights to arrive in groups. This way, comparisons can be drawn, common themes can be discovered, winners can be rewarded and losers knocked soundly over the head. Stragglers aren't welcome; they clog the overview.

Usefully, the mood is changing. These days so many playwrights are writing so well, and so differently from each other, that it really isn't possible to categorise them. From a present-day perspective, Terry Johnson can be seen as a nineties maverick who just happened to arrive a couple of decades early. And it's equally possible, now, to see him within a much older theatrical tradition; that of English Puritanism. This is the tradition of a handful of playwrights of the pre-Civil War era: Webster, Tourneur and, in particular, Thomas Middleton. Their theme, like Johnson's, was sex as a universal human obsession. What makes this obsession a fatal one – in the Puritan cosmology – is not guilt or the threat of damnation, neither of which, after all, has any rational basis. It is the fact that, in flesh, sex shares a common denominator with death.

Terry Johnson deals obsessively with this starkly Puritan theme, though his treatment of it is always comedic. The fact that his comedy *works* – that the audience laughs immoderately at precisely the points he's planned – says a lot about his fascination with the mechanics of comedy and even more about his mastery of them, but it doesn't undermine the bleakness of his vision. Laughter in adults is generally a function of terror, shame or *schadenfreude*: it seldom has much to do with happiness. And laughter in Johnson's plays is ironic, even a touch grotesque: it's like a pair of inverted commas within which a highly Jacobean masque of mortality is acted out.

Each of the plays in this volume has a death at its centre. And in each, a different comedy idiom is provided as 'frame'. The frame in *Imagine Drowning* is the weirdest of the three: it's a lowbrow genre for which I know no name. 'English Macabre'? It has its fullest expression for some reason in seaside resorts, in the shape of freak shows, malformed foetuses in bottles, waxworks featuring instruments of torture, and those miniature Haunted Houses, beloved of my childhood, where a gloomy but comatose room burst into life the moment you put a penny in the slot. Coffin lids creaked open, ghosts peeped in the window and cupboard doors swung wide revealing lines of blood-stained murder instruments, very much as Brenda's living-room secretes hamsters, a bouncing head and a grisly past.

The juxtaposition of eternality and tat is what's so curious about the seaside, and Johnson makes much of this; on a divided stage, a few footsteps separate the haunted house from the beach, the tides and the wide horizon. Here Buddy the moon-walker, standing in as it were for the moon itself, acts as witness and healer.

At the heart of the play is a blankness and a vast depression. 'How can we ever know? Our loved ones' asked David in the brilliant cross-talk passage half-way through Act Two. 'Never', says Jane. But it's not a reply; she and he are inhabiting different time-zones, so even this brief moment of communication – or potential 'knowing' of each other – is denied them. The play's title is ambiguous. Its meaning turns on whether you think that 'drowning' is intransitive – as it seems the first time you look at it – or transitive; that the drowning is being done by you to somebody else. If the latter, it's a warning; imagine drowning the person you love, as you very well might. Murder (says the play) isn't the preserve of tabloid monsters; every sexual relationship harbours the murderous impulse to some degree. 'That sticky black darkness! It's in us all for Christ's sake, isn't it?'

The title of *Hysteria* comes packed with echoes: hysterical laughter, nineteenth-century psychiatric diagnosis, the womb. This Freudian deathbed fantasia works so dazzlingly well in performance that it seems a shame to pick it apart, but *not* to analyse it would be paradoxical, given the subject matter.

The comic idiom this time is English farce, this being of all art forms the one which revels most in Freudian slips. (The great farce line of all time was given by Ray Cooney to an outraged hotelier: 'There's too much sex going on in this hotel! And I'm *not having it!*') The basic farcical image of a door flying open to reveal a tableau of sexual guilt is neatly equated with the psychoanalytic process, in which an identical phenomenon so often occurs.

Ruthlessly exploited is Freud's ambivalence towards mystique: mine is fascinating, anyone else's is superstitious twaddle. A particular scene, described by Jung in his memoirs, is quite good enough to appear in *Hysteria*. (It almost does.) He and Freud were discussing paranormal phenomena. Freud stoutly refuted their existence: the atmosphere grew tense. Suddenly a loud bang was heard from a bookcase. 'What is that?' exclaimed Freud, caught off-balance. 'That,' replied Jung, speaking on some impulse which mystified him even as he spoke, 'is a catalytic exteriorisation phenomenon. And, what's more, I predict it will happen again.' Freud hardly had time to arrange his features into stern disbelief before the bookcase emanated a second loud bang. 'That,' Jung was later to reflect, 'marked the first cooling in our relationship.' Most Johnsonian about *Hysteria* is the way in which sexual capering – hilarious to the onlooker, demeaning for the caperer – conveys the pathos of the human animal when stripped, as Freud insists it must be, of belief in God. Is man no more than this? A poor, bare, forked animal with a bulging erection? (Or 'a squidgy single-minded probiscus', as Jessica unkindly puts it.)

The introduction of Dali is potentially explosive: in his painstaking replication of the surreal he so clearly mirrors the playwright. Johnson boldly exposes him to masterly put-down at the hands of Freud: 'When I look at your work I'm afraid all I see is what is conscious . . . The conscious rendition of conscious thoughts. You murder dreams.' One thinks of Hitchcock's *Spellbound*, with its deadening Dali landscapes. But Johnson's surreal devices are funny and full of life.

The first of Terry Johnson's comedies *about* comedy, *Unsuitable for Adults*, took both its setting and its comic idiom from the alternative comedy circuit of the mid-eighties. *Dead Funny* is his second: the idiom this time is the leering, childish and generally reprehensible television comedy of the sixties, the characters (bar one) its fans. Richard, Brian, Nick and Lisa, in their 'upmarket area bordering on city suburbs' are slaves of comedy, slaves of sex, condemned, when groping, fondling and lying to each other, to do so in the form of Benny Hill, Jeremy Hawke and sundry long forgotten blondes. In Webster or Toureur, a skull would have lurked as a memento mori; here, a Victorian medical human torso spills its guts on to the carpet. 'I'll give you a permanent bloody sense of your own mortality' shouts Eleanor, trying to get her husband to tidy up.

What a pleasure it is to introduce a twentieth-century Jacobean; original, tragic, a charnel-house joker. Welcome to Death's Jest Book.

Nicholas Wright
London 1998

# Imagine Drowning

**Imagine Drowning** was premièred at the Hampstead Theatre on 24 January 1991 with the following cast:

| | |
|---|---|
| **Jane** | Sylvestra le Touzel |
| **Brenda** | Frances Barber |
| **Tom** | Nabil Shaban |
| **David** | Douglas Hodge |
| **Buddy** | Ed Bishop |
| **Sam** | Daniel Evans |

*Directed by* Richard Wilson
*Designed by* Julian McGowan
*Lighting by* Rick Fisher

## Characters

**Jane**  *Late twenties. County origins. A veneer of sophistication that only just hides her vulnerability.*

**Brenda**  *Late thirties. Cumbrian. A very slow woman, and quite uneducated. At times one might think her a little retarded, but that only reflects the degree to which she has chosen to participate in the world.*

**Tom**  *A substantially disabled man in his thirties. Very active. Very articulate.*

**David**  *Early thirties. Londoner. A tall, attractive man with a dark, brooding quality. He takes himself very seriously.*

**Buddy**  *A middle-aged middle-American. Softly spoken, quite self-absorbed.*

**Sam**  *Brenda's son. Under fifteen. All the attendant physical problems of the adolescent.*

**Sophie**  *Brenda's daughter. As young as possible.*

## Setting

*A guest house near Gosforth in Cumbria. Beyond and around it; the shore, a barren coastline.*

*The front room has been knocked through to the back. The front door and staircase are visible, maybe the upstairs landing. Enough steps, doors, corners, nooks and crannies to give the impression of the classical haunted house transported to this specific time and location.*

*A few years ago, the house might have called itself a hotel. Now, it's hard to imagine any traveller staying more than one night.*

*The living room furnishings are faded, autumnal. A ruinous, saggy three-piece suite and other chairs all arranged with an easy view of the TV.*

*The TV is enormous.*

*The back of the VACANCIES/NO VACANCIES sign hanging in the window. An incongruous payphone.*

*A hatch to the kitchen, and under the stairs an old DIY attempt at a checking-in desk.*

*Toys litter the carpet.*

*There are only two strange signs of affluence; a video recorder and a complete set of* The Encyclopaedia Britannica.

*The room is also full to the brim with pets, or evidence of them. A cage for gerbils, a cage for mice. Two large aquaria with tubes and filters and paraphernalia. A budgie cage with too many budgies in it. A none-too-healthy parrot. Dog basket, cat litter.*

# *Act One*

## Prologue

*In the darkness, the Song of the Whale.*

*The aquaria light up, then the television (an undersea wildlife programme), then the rest of it. Greens and blues and motion that suggests deep water.*

*The characters are revealed in this submerged world. The swell of the water puts them in motion; small repeated gestures suggest images from the play we are about to see.*

*The lights change and* **Buddy** *appears on the beach with a lit paper moon, which he stakes into the sand.*

**Buddy** Grounded. Worse. Sent to England. To witness a sort of drowning. At first I was teaching young men to duck and weave through Cumbrian hills; less of an expert than an inspiration to those boys. And believe me, the morale of those young pilots from California and Kentucky had reached a pretty low ebb in and around Penrith, in England, in the late eighties, in the rain. So, having no further use for this particular brand of hero at home they shipped me over to remind those bored young bucks that even if they had decided on short acquaintance that the miserable English were really not worth defending, they were, like me, the US Airforce, and should be proud to fly over any godforsaken maniacally depressed country they were told to. And I counted those boys lucky, for they could do what I no longer could. They could fly. It had been decided that my flying days were long gone. I knew this, but the grey slate and the thumping rain to an earthbound soul made the earth unbearable. Briefly, I took to the bottle. Briefly. Then I took to the beach. They stood me down, I turned down their offer to fly me home again, and gave myself up to the magnetic pull of this magnificent shoreline. I tell you all this to explain my presence which in a practical sense is improbable. My own drama having played itself out twenty years ago, my role in this one was to be purely metaphysical. I knew nothing of its early scenes, except to be familiar with the dark and dreary boarding house that stood at the end of the esplanade. This was Brenda's house. She lived there with her children and her lodger Tom, who started the whole thing with some inadvisable call to the press. But this is not Tom's story, nor Brenda's (though you may have heard hers elsewhere). This is the story of Jane and David, who arrived on this bleak north-western coast two weeks apart, Jane looking for David, David looking for something even less tangible than himself. You could, I suppose, if you chose, ignore the rest of us. We are merely the Other People.

Scene One

*Lights up on the living room.* **Brenda** *alone, watching TV, 'This Is Your Life'.*

*The doorbell rings.* **Brenda** *uses the remote control to turn the TV down and answers the door. It's raining out.* **Jane** *is therefore sopping wet.*

**Jane** Hello.

**Brenda** Hello.

*A pause*

**Jane** I'm looking for a room.

**Brenda** (*very serious. Nods*) Mmm.

**Jane** I'm very wet.

**Brenda** You'd better come in.

**Jane** I might make a bit of a puddle, I'm sorry. Does it always rain this hard?

**Brenda** Yes, it's the weather.

**Brenda** *is neither welcoming nor hostile. She seems unused to guests.*

**Jane** Have you a room available?

**Brenda** Well, it is very quiet.

**Jane** Time of year I suppose?

**Brenda** No.

*Pause.*

**Brenda** We like it.

**Jane** What?

**Brenda** Quiet.

**Jane** Oh. I shan't be staying for long.

**Brenda** Holiday is it?

**Jane** No. Well, yes. See the sights.

**Brenda** Where?

**Jane** Well, do some walking. Nowhere in particular.

**Brenda** Well, the world's your lobster, isn't it?

**Jane** The world's my what?

**Brenda** Not lobster.

**Jane** Oyster.

**Brenda** That's it. Funny sort of fish for the world to be. You're meant to sign something. This is a sort of desk like a hotel if you do this. Feel silly. But you have to. There's a book somewhere. To sign. There's cotton sheets. Gas is all in no meter.

**Jane** Sea view?

**Brenda** No. Here we are then.

**Brenda** *opens the book.* **Jane** *signs.* **Brenda** *laughs a little laugh.*

**Brenda** Haven't had a Mz before. That means you're not married, does it?

**Jane***'s fingers move spontaneously to cover her wedding finger, on which is no ring.*

**Jane** No. No, it means it doesn't matter if I am or not.

**Brenda** Oh. I see.

**Brenda***'s hand covers her own ring finger, which* has *got a ring on it.*

**Brenda** It's a double bed.

**Jane** I'm on my own.

**Brenda** I'll go and put the sheets on. And the fire, take the chill out. You sit down here and get yourself warm. Make yourself at home. It's only a living room if there's no one. When there's someone it's the Television Lounge. You can watch the telly. Would you like to watch the telly?

**Jane** No thanks.

**Brenda** You can.

**Jane** Thanks. No.

**Brenda** Switch it off shall I?

**Jane** No, whatever.

**Brenda** 'This Is Your Life'.

**Jane** I see.

**Brenda** *stops still and watches. Television tends to mesmerize her.*

**Jane** Do you mind if I make a phone call?

**Brenda** Oh, I'm sorry. Please, do. I'll put a bottle in, just in case.

**Brenda** *goes upstairs and* **Jane** *goes to the phone.*

**Brenda** Give it a bang.

**Jane** *bangs the phone. The parrot is nearby.*

**Parrot** Hello.

*She decides not to answer. Dials.*

**Parrot** Do you love me? Do you? Do you love me?

**Jane** Mummy. It's me. / Yes, I know, I'm sorry. / I'm not coming. / No, I'm fine. I'm fine. I'm just not coming. / I am phoning. / I wasn't near a phone. I was on a train. / Cumbria. / I got a postcard from him. / Mummy, I know you'd be much happier if he was dead and gone but he's not. He's just . . . gone, somewhere, I don't know. I'll phone you soon. Well, put it in the deep freeze. / Well, mince it up for rissoles or something.

*A small but very grotesque monster pokes its head around a corner.*

**Jane** Mummy, don't start. Look, I'm in a box; there are people waiting. / No, I'm perfectly alright. Mummy, I am perfectly safe!

*She sees the monster and screams. It comes in and sits on the sofa. Reads a comic.*

**Jane** No, it's alright. I'm alright. I'm fine. No. Nothing. It was just a spider on the thingummy, that's all. You know what I'm like. / Yes I will. I promise. / Mummy, I promise. If I get murdered I'll call you, now bye bye.

*She puts the phone down.*

**Jane** You know, if I had a face like that, I'd wear a mask.

**Brenda** *returns.*

**Brenda** Sam! I told you. Bedroom.

*He goes.*

**Brenda** Thought you might like this.

**Jane** Thank you.

*Hands* **Jane** *a towel for her hair.* **Jane** *dries it,* **Brenda** *watches.*

**Brenda** And I've put the kettle on. Would you like a cup of tea?

**Jane** I'd love a cup of tea. Er, before you go . . . this postcard.

**Brenda** Yes?

**Jane** It's a photograph of this house, isn't it?

**Brenda** It's the esplanade. That's what they used to call it, when people came.

**Jane** My husband sent this to me. That's his writing.

**Brenda** Wish you were here. Ha ha. What does that mean then; ha ha?

**Jane** He has a funny sense of humour. He always sends me a postcard. I took this to the photographer's; their name is

printed on the back. They directed me here. My husband's
name is David Sinclair. David Sinclair. Do you know him?

**Brenda** No.

**Jane** This is his picture.

**Brenda** No.

**Jane** Are you sure?

**Brenda** Yes, I'm sure.

**Jane** He sent me this postcard. Are you absolutely positive?

**Brenda** No. I mean, yes. I mean I've never seen him in my
life, no.

**Jane** It would only have been a couple of weeks ago. He's a
journalist.

**Brenda** I'm sorry.

**Jane** Damn. If I hadn't come so far I'd turn right round and
go back.

**Brenda** Yes. I would if I had.

**Jane** I'll die of pneumonia if I don't get out of these things.

**Brenda** Your room's at the top of the stairs. First on the left.
I'll bring you up the tea?

**Jane** No, it's alright. I'll come down.

**Jane** *picks up her suitcase and goes upstairs. Kettle boils offstage.*
**Brenda** *leaves. The doorbell rings.* **Brenda** *returns, without her*
*cardigan on. Opens the door. Bright evening sunshine.* **David** *is at*
*the door.*

(AS WELL AS BEING WITH **Jane**, WE SHALL SPEND TIME WITH
**David** ON HIS VISIT A FEW WEEKS EARLIER. THE QUALITY OF
LIGHT IS ALL THAT INDICATES THIS DOUBLE TIME SCHEME.)

**David** Hello. Does um, Tom Dudgeon live here?

**Brenda** Um.

**David** My name's David Sinclair. I was given this address.

**Brenda** Oh, Yes. He's not in.

**David** Oh. It says on the window vacancies. Does that mean there's a room I could . . .

**Brenda** What?

**David** Stay in?

**Brenda** Oh. Of course. Yes. You'll have to sign the book.

**David** Fine. Will he be back soon?

**Brenda** Never know with Tom.

**David** Is there a phone?

**Brenda** A pippy phone.

**David** In the room?

**Brenda** Over there.

**David** Right.

*He goes to the phone.*

**Brenda** Give it a bang.

*He does, then dials.*

**Brenda** Will you be wanting breakfast?

**David** Oh, coffee, croissant.

**Brenda** Yes. How many eggs?

**David** Alright, two.

**Brenda** Bacon, sausage and tomatoes. Full English breakfast.

**David** Delicious. Hello, Bob? It's David. / I'm in Cumbria.

**Brenda** *leaves.*

**David** Cornwall? No, I came north. Edge of nowhere. / What the hell ever happens in Cornwall? / Oh, send Stuart; I can't make Cornwall, I'm in bloody Cumbria. / I did tell the office. I told Tish. / Bob, you didn't have a story for me and when this guy called you were still out to lunch. / I don't know yet. Some sort of protest at Sellafield. / Tomorrow morning, first thing. I did what I thought you'd want me to do! / Look, this is ridiculous. Are you seriously suggesting I take the milk train to cover Her Majesty the Prime Minister opening another fucking ring road? I could do that from here, for Christ's sake. / Bob, do you know how far away Plymouth is? / I know trains run all night, they're where I usually sleep. / Alright. I'll get the bloody train. But when a gang of maniacs cut the wire and go apeshit in Sellafield and my arse is in Cornwall, you can kiss it.

*Puts the phone down. Dials again.*

**Parrot** Hello.

**David** *ignores it. Phone is answered.*

**David** Hello?

**Parrot** Hello.

**David** Fuck off. Hello? Can you put me through to Andrew Norris please. (*To* **Parrot**.) Fuck off. Come on, after me. Fuck off. Fuck off.

**Parrot** Fuck off!

**David** Well done. Andrew? David. / Sinclair. Listen Andy, I'm calling in that favour. I want you to file a story for me. / Thatcher opening the ring road. / Andy, you don't have to be there. Just type up the first agency report, snide reference to the quality of life on the M25, and put my name on it. / I might not be near a phone. I'm having a sniff around something. As a matter of fact, yes. / Wouldn't you like to know. Just cover my bum, will you? / Thank you, Andrew. Quits. Bye.

**David** *sees a pile of postcards on the desk-flap.*

**Brenda** *enters with a towel.*

**Brenda** Here's a towel, it's included.

**David** Are these of here?

**Brenda** Yes.

**David** Seen better days.

**Brenda** I know.

*He takes a postcard.*

**Brenda** For the animals.

**David** What?

*She lifts and junkles her RSPCA collection box.*

**David** Oh.

*He donates. She gives him the key.*

**David** See you later then.

**Brenda** Yes. Will you be staying long?

**David** Only tonight.

*He picks up his suitcase and word processor and goes upstairs.*

*Kettle boils offstage.* **Brenda** *disappears briefly and returns with her cardigan on and a tray of tea.*

**Jane** *descends.*

**Jane** It's a lovely room.

**Brenda** (*Surprised*) Is it alright?

**Jane** And there is a sea view.

**Brenda** No.

**Jane** If you stand on tiptoe and look out of the top window, between the roofs, a little blue triangle.

**Brenda** Well I never.

**Jane** Well, grey, a very small triangle.

**Brenda** I was going to say. I'd have noticed that. Here we are then. Lovely cup of tea.

**Parrot** Lovely cup of tea.

**Brenda** Cheeky devil.

**Jane** (*Smiles*) What's his name?

**Brenda** Moby Dick.

**Jane** Isn't that a fish?

**Brenda** No, a cockatoo.

**Jane** You like animals?

**Brenda** I love animals.

**Jane** *finds a perspex thingummy on the mantelpiece.*

**Jane** What's this?

**Brenda** Ant farm.

**Jane** Eurgh. Where are the ants?

**Brenda** Don't know. Sam left the top off.

**Jane** Highly sophisticated social order, ants.

*She sits on the sofa.*

**Brenda** All buggered off in a long line across the carpet. There's a hamster too, somewhere. In the sofa probably.

**Jane** *gets up from the sofa.*

**Jane** What's in here?

**Brenda** Gerbils. Don't lift the lid.

**Jane** I wasn't going to.

**Brenda** Gerbils jump.

**Jane** You don't let them out then?

**Brenda** Well, Sophie's not allowed to play with the gerbils. She loves them too hard. Sends them bye byes. And they stay a bye byes until I can get down the petshop.

**Jane** You should try to explain it to her, surely.

**Brenda** What?

**Jane** Death.

**Brenda** I didn't know there was an explanation.

**Jane** *starts to cry.*

**Jane** Sorry. This is stupid. I'm just very tired. He never phoned. His paper doesn't care; he let them down on something or other. His editor suggested I look in the nearest gutter. I've been to the police. He doesn't qualify as a missing person, until he turns up dead or something, I don't know. All I've got is this stupid bloody postcard. Sorry.

**Brenda** He never came home? Your husband?

**Jane** No.

**Brenda** *crosses herself.*

**Jane** Was he here?

**Brenda** I have tried with Sophie. I tried to tell her why we had to bury the rabbit. She understood until Friday then dug it up again to see if it was hungry. No, nothing dies in this house. They just change colour. 'Mummy, why is Moby Dick white when he was green yesterday?' Because he had his feathers changed, my love. He had a change of heart.

*She goes to the parrot.* Tell me you love me.

**Parrot** *gives a low rumbling squawk.*

**Brenda** Do you?

**Parrot** Love you.

**Brenda** *smiles at* **Jane**.

**Jane** Thanks for the tea.

**Jane** *goes upstairs.*

*The weather changes.*

*A key in the lock and* **Tom** *enters in his wheelchair with a bag full of loofahs.*

**Brenda** Tom?

**Tom** Only me.

**Brenda** Tom, there's a man.

**Tom** Is there?

**Brenda** Yes. There is. There's a man to see you. Who is he, Tom?

**Tom** Until I meet him, Brenda, it's hard for me to say. Here.

*He hands her a small package.*

**Brenda** What is it?

**Tom** For the children.

**Brenda** What is it?

**Tom** Guess.

**Brenda** Water wings.

**Tom** That's astonishing.

**Brenda** I'm right?

**Tom** No, you're completely wrong. But so was I. I thought it was water wings too. Blow it up.

**Brenda** *inflates the gift. It is a globe of the earth in coloured vinyl plastic.*

**Tom** I bought it without looking. I had no idea. Don't let her use it in the water. If she lost her grip she could drown.

**Brenda** It's beautiful, Tom. It's not water wings, no. But it's beautiful.

**David** *comes downstairs.*

**David** Sorry. Hello. Is there a pub?

**Brenda** This is the man, Tom.

**David** Tom? Tom Dudgeon?

**Tom** Hello.

**David** Hello. Sorry. David Sinclair.

**Tom** Pleased to meet you. This is Brenda.

**David** We've met.

**Brenda** Hello.

**David** Hello.

*Pause.*

**David** Are there any sheets?

**Brenda** Sheets?

**David** For the bed.

**Brenda** Oh, I'm sorry. I'm so, so sorry.

**David** That's alright.

**Brenda** I'm so terribly sorry.

**Tom** Brenda.

**Brenda** What?

**Tom** Don't castigate yourself.

**Brenda** No. What?

**Tom** Just put some sheets on the bed.

**Brenda** Right. (*Whispers to* **David**.) I'm sorry, really. I am so sorry.

**David** It's alright, really.

*She leaves.* **Tom** *takes loofahs out of the bag and piles them on a table.*

**Tom** Thanks for coming.

**David** It had better be worth it.

**Tom** The only newspaper in this town is strictly weddings and netball.

**David** You said there was going to be a demonstration. How big?

**Tom** Pretty big for these parts.

**David** Outside the plant?

**Tom** Where else?

**David** Inside?

**Tom** Perhaps. I'll give you a lift out there in the morning.

**Brenda** *comes back with sheets.*

**David** Thank you. What in?

**Tom** I drive a mini.

**Brenda** Tom's a very good driver.

**David** Well, you'd have to be, I suppose. Is there a pub?

**Tom** Just down the road.

**David** Could we talk there?

**Tom** Certainly.

**David** I'll get my notebook.

**David** *leaves*.

**Brenda** Who is he, Tom?

**Tom** It's alright, Brenda.

**Brenda** Works for the papers.

**Tom** For the good papers. I need him. Don't worry yourself.

**Brenda** Trust you.

**Tom** Yes. You can.

**David** *comes downstairs.* **Brenda** *goes into the kitchen.*

**David** Why me, anyway?

**Tom** How many good left-wing journalists are there?

**David** You know the paper I work for has just changed hands? Assurances of editorial freedom of course, but I can't guarantee they'll print anything unless you hack a copper to death.

**Tom** That bad?

**David** Getting worse.

**Tom** Will you resign?

**David** No. Time was.

**Tom** What changed?

**David** I did.

*They leave.*

**Jane** *comes downstairs quietly. Looks in the register.*

**Brenda** *enters from the kitchen wheeling* **Tom**. *He carries a tea tray.*

**Jane** *closes the book hurriedly.*

**Brenda** Oh.

**Jane** Hello. I was um . . .

**Brenda** This is Tom. This is the woman, Tom.

**Tom** Hello.

**Jane** Hello.

**Tom** My impersonation of a tea trolley.

**Jane** Very good.

**Tom** Thank you.

**Brenda** *pours.*

**Tom** Welcome to Cumbria.

**Jane** Thank you.

**Tom** Brenda tells me you're looking for a man.

**Jane** I'm looking for my husband. David Sinclair.

**Tom** Is he blind?

**Jane** Blind? No.

**Tom** Only David Sinclair I knew was blind. Met him in disabled school. It was a lot of fun having him push my chair about. None of the staff thought it was much fun, but the spazzers cheered up no end. 'Left hand down a bit, David!' Crash. He was deaf in one ear, you see.

**Jane** Yes. I see.

**Tom** He once asked me to describe the moon to him. That was depressing. Not because I failed but because his curiosity was infectious. What must it be like? Riding about on those leggy things you've all got. Lurching along, masters of your ship, not lashed to the wheel. Whatever the weather, at one with those two tree-trunk galleons.

**Jane** Yes. I um . . .

**Brenda** You don't want to listen to Tom. There's something wrong with his cephalic index, that's what it is.

**Jane** Oh, I'm sorry.

**Tom** Taught me a lot did David's curiosity.

**Jane** Discontent?

**Tom** Imagination.

**Brenda** Oh, imagination. I sometimes wish I had that. Just imagine.

**Jane** Two weeks ago my David went off on the assignment and that's the last I saw of him.

**Tom** Have you tried the police?

**Jane** They told me to wait ten days.

**Tom** Ten days?

**Jane** Length of a cheap package holiday. But he's not abroad. He came north, I'm sure of that.

**Tom** Well, he didn't stay here.

**Jane** You are sure?

**Tom** Why should we lie? Have you been married long?

**Jane** Four years. Why?

**Tom** Happy ever after?

**Jane** He stayed somewhere in this town. Tomorrow I'll try the other hotels.

**Tom** Shouldn't take you long.

**Jane** (*rises, stops*) Is there a pub?

**Tom** Other side of town.

**Jane** I'll find him if it kills me.

*Grabs her coat and leaves.*

**Brenda** Tom . . .

**Tom** Shhh. Cephalic index?

**Brenda** It's a real word.

**Tom** I'm impressed.

**Brenda** I'd rather have an Imagination. If I did I'd do all sorts of things in my head. Skiing. Snow. Drive a car.

**Tom** Climb a ladder.

**Brenda** In a forest with monkeys.

*Stops, embarrassed.*

**Tom** Go on.

**Brenda** Go in a cave. Find a four leaf clover. Looked though. Play the piano. Whatsit, banjo. Ghost train.

**Tom** Easy. Just climb on.

**Brenda** No. I never could. I've picked flowers. But smoked salmon.

**Tom** What?

**Brenda** In Safeways.

**Tom** Smoked salmon?

**Brenda** I almost though. Lots of times.

**Tom** Go on.

**Brenda** I couldn't. Never even done cat's cradle. When I was small. Brought it home, cat's cradle. Couldn't do it. Got my fingers tangled. Got all tangled up.

**Brenda** *panics.*

**Brenda** Tom. . .!

**Tom** It's alright.

**Brenda** But she . . . what if she . . .

**Tom** It's OK. It's alright. He's gone.

**Brenda** He might have . . .

**Tom** He might have got a little bit wet, that's all.

*Pause.*

**Brenda** Oh Tom. Listen to that rain.

*Lights fade.*


Scene Two

*Evening.* **Tom** *and* **David** *arrive from the pub.* **David** *is drunk.*

**David** When the really bad news began . . . South Africa, 1985, I was there. My first serious foreign assignment. If they'd known how serious it was going to get they'd have sent someone older. Someone like Stephenson. He was there; this Fleet Street legend, pissed old cynic, I hated him. When the worst started there were twelve of us in a hotel television lounge sending out the most fantastic stuff. A dozen of us yelling down the only three phone lines. Runners coming in with eye-witnesses. A fourteen-year-old boy dripping blood on my word-processor, I remember, wouldn't go wash up, wanted to tell us, wanted us to tell. The din, the adrenalin. You've never felt anything like it. Then four days later the lines were down, metaphorically I mean. Everything was D notice. It piled up until we stopped collecting. Material that would have made a dozen colour supplements, let alone the actual news, and no way to pass it out without the actual risk of actual arrest, and – we had the evidence – of actual torture. I was desperate to get this stuff out, but after a couple of days the hotel lounge had come to a full stop. All these so called foreign correspondents sitting around drinking iced coffee. Only topic of conversation seemed to be where to get your laundry done. Stephenson sat there. He could see I was furious.

He put down his glass, and said, 'You hear that noise?'
'What noise?'
It was silent as the grave.
I said, 'What noise?'
He looked at the dead typewriters and the comatose phones and he said, 'The silence. Do you know what that silence is?'
I said no.
He said, 'Genocide. The silence is genocide.'

**Tom** You used that line. I remember reading that.

**David** It's a very good line. Tight, perceptive, emotive. It had the desired effect on me. I exploded. A torrent of righteous indignation. How dare we all just fucking sit there! We are the voice of these people. It's our job to break the silence! Stephenson smiled, and passed me the phone. We had been forbidden to ask for an outside line. We both knew I might be arrested. Silenced. And I did not have the courage to pick up that phone. And I knew that my life up until that moment had been rhetoric. That whatever I believed or said or said I believed . . . it was just words. I was what mattered. The only really important thing in my life was me.

I once interviewed Enoch Powell. He was defending strong government. He said he believed that man was primarily self-centred, thus incurably greedy and inevitably violent to his fellow man. I said wasn't that a pretty pessimistic view of humanity?

He said, 'Of course. I'm a pessimist. That's why I'm a Tory.'

*A physical display of anger from* **David**. *Pent up, unexpressable.*

**Tom** Why does that upset you so much?

**David** I'm a pessimist too. I find it hard to imagine a world without winners and losers. It's like pissing in the wind trying to help the blacks, the unemployed, the crippled, sorry, the disenchanted, disenfranchised, the bloody Rainbow Alliance for Christ's sake; the losing side . . . Oh, battles have been won, revolutions have been staged to reorganise the corruption . . . but for 10,000 years the losers have fought and lost and lived and lost and lost and lost again . . . Socialism didn't die last week; it never drew its first breath.

**Tom** Stalin saw to that. True socialism . . .

**David** Is a dream!

**Tom** Well, capitalism's a fucking nightmare.

**David** It was never real! Reality isn't what we hope for or work for or imagine. Reality is the concrete world we live in. Reality is solid. This is reality.

*He bangs his fist on the coffee table. It collapses.*

**David** Shit.

**Tom** Nothing's certain. There are no immovable objects, no irresistible forces.

**David** *takes some volumes of* The Encyclopaedia Britannica *and props up the table.*

**Tom** What are you doing?

**David** I'm mending the table.

**Tom** It'll never be good as new. Second Law of Thermodynamics. The table's doomed to wobble from now on. Eventually it'll all fall down.

**David** Bollocks. There you go. Solid as a rock.

**Tom** Revolution is the only viable alternative. A new table.

**Tom** *throws* **David** *the globe.* **David** *heads for the stairs with it.*

**David** Then what? Who sits around the table? Who gets to eat at the fucking table?

**Tom** Why are you angry at me? Be angry at them.

**David** There's a bit of them in all of us, God knows! I can feel it. Can't you feel it? A black and bloody nugget in us all.

*He has gone.*

**Tom** *goes to the dining table and begins painting a placard in red paint, which will eventually read 'SOUTH AFRICAN BLOOD BATH'.* **Jane** *arrives through the front door with a bottle of Scotch.*

**Tom** Hello.

**Jane** You startled me.

**Tom** Only said hello.

**Jane** I don't usually drink. Didn't want to die of pneumonia.

**Tom** Worse things to die of. Found him yet?

**Jane** No.

**Tom** Town this size, if you haven't yet you're not likely to.

**Jane** You sound as if you don't much care.

**Tom** Why should I?

**Jane** You're very rude. Have a drink.

**Tom** Go to bed.

**Jane** Just a small one.

**Tom** I am the envy of many alcoholics, being legless even before my first drink, which means my alcohol level is well above the brain before you can say Jack Daniels. So if I drank with you I'd end up on the carpet, and you'd have to pick me up and take me beddybyes.

*He waggles his tongue lasciviously.*

**Jane** You don't like me, do you?

**Tom** Go to bed.

**Jane** It's very hard to talk with you.

**Tom** You should try dancing.

**Jane** I keep feeling I ought to be polite all the time, but you don't deserve it. You're not polite. In fact, you're not even very nice.

**Tom** Don't be silly. Disabled people are extremely nice. I haven't always been like this. I was a Buddhist monk in a previous incarnation.

**Jane** What happened?

**Tom** I must have raped a nun or something. Fucked it right up, anyway. I wish I'd re-incarnated in the East. I would have been treated like a minor deity, not shit on wheels.

**Jane** I've treated you like a perfectly normal person.

**Tom** Well you'd have to. This one's *articulate* shit on wheels. Step on me, I not only mess up your shoe, I also criticise your taste in footwear.

**Jane** I do think you're very brave.

**Tom** Oh Christ. Look, I moved north to get away from platitudes like that. Up here there are no disabled toilets but there are plenty of blokes who'll throw me over their shoulder and carry me in.

**Jane** I spend my life apologising for not being working-class.

**Tom** God, give me strength.

**Jane** But if you insist on being so damn superior . . .

**Tom** I just can't stand it when people . . .

**Jane** Then people are going to be superior back at you.

**Tom** . . . 'make an effort'.

**Jane** Yes I was. But for my sake, not yours. I need a friend.

**Tom** And presumably so does the physically handicapped person.

**Jane** I give up.

**Parrot** Hello.

**Jane** Hello.

**Parrot** Do you love me?

**Jane** I hardly know you. Do you love me? Say I love you. Come on. I love you. Tell me, I love you.

**Parrot** Fuck off.

**Jane** *is inordinately upset.*

**Tom** Are you alright?

**Jane** What upsets me is how you sit there . . . liking yourself so much. I mean, I'm a very nice person. I am. And I fucking hate me. God, I'm pissed.

**Parrot** *squawks.*

**Jane** Oh, fuck off yourself.

**Tom** Did you tell David to fuck off?

**Jane** No I fucking didn't because I don't fucking swear. Who taught a nice innocent creature disgusting words like that?

**Tom** I don't know.

**Jane** David swore. When I met him he was the most articulate man I ever met. Just before he left all I ever heard was f this, bugger that, sod you.

**Tom** It's late. I'm off to bed. Busy day tomorrow.

*He goes towards his room.*

**Jane** There's a pub just around the corner. You said the nearest pub was across the town. Why did you say that?

**Tom** Had to get you out of the house.

**Jane** Why?

**Tom** Hide the body.

**Jane** Ha. Ha.

*He has gone. She drinks, shivers. Goes back to the register, but is interrupted again by a thump from the top of the stairs.*

**Jane** Who's there?

*She goes to the stairs to investigate. No one. Turns to walk away. A man's head comes bumping down the stair. She stifles a scream.* **Sam** *laughs from upstairs. She investigates the head. It's rubber, faintly recognisable as* **David**.

**Sam** *runs downstairs, picks up the head, and runs back to bed.*

**Sam** Were you scared?

**Jane** Yes thank you.

*He goes. She drinks. Lights fade.*


Scene Three

*Lights come up for the next morning.* **Tom** *is very busy.* **Jane** *runs down the stairs for breakfast.*

**Jane** Good morning.

**Tom** Good morning. You're too late.

**Jane** For what?

**Tom** Breakfast.

**Jane** That's alright, I couldn't.

**Tom** I need your help.

**Jane** What sort of help?

**Tom** We're going shopping. We'll need this, this and this.

*He hands her a can of red paint, a screwdriver and a large handwritten notice that says 'SOUTH AFRICAN BLOODBATH'.*

**Jane** Why? What?

**Tom** I need you to wheel me to the doorway of Sainsbury's, dump me, then wheel the chair away and out of sight. If the law show up before you've made your move, abort the mission. If they show up later keep your head down and get as many photos as you can.

*He hands her a camera.*

**Jane** I take dreadful photos. I cut people's heads off.

**Tom** Then you'll probably get me centre frame.

**Jane** Well no, really, actually I feel a bit sick.

**Brenda** *comes in with* **Jane***'s breakfast.*

**Brenda** Full English breakfast.

**Jane** Oh God. Thank you.

**Brenda** Are you going out, Tom?

**Tom** Yes.

**Brenda** Are you coming back or will you be at the police station again?

**Tom** Not sure.

**Brenda** I'll do a salad.

**Brenda** *exits.*

**Jane** Are you going to do something illegal?

**Tom** (*yells*) The fruit in this store was grown on stolen land!

**Jane** God, my head.

**Tom** The tinned fruit was canned by black slave labour!

**Jane** Tom, please.

**Tom** The money you pay for it directly funds the oppression of the black South African majority!

**Jane** Please. Save the world if you must, but do it quietly. I can't eat this.

*She goes to the kitchen.* **David** *comes downstairs.*

**Tom** Get your anti-nuclear loofahs here! Get yourself well scrubbed. Reaches the parts other decontaminating agents cannot reach. Get your anti-nuclear loofah here!

**David** Shut up for Christ's sake.

**Tom** Good morning.

**David** You know why the Russian revolution failed? Vodka. That's why the Russian revolution failed.

*Enter* **Brenda** *with more breakfast.*

**Brenda** Full English breakfast.

**Brenda** *exits.* **David** *looks at breakfast.*

**David** Don't suppose it's time to go, is it?

**Tom** If you like.

**David** I need some fresh air.

**Tom** I'll follow you. Take this.

*Gives* **David** *the bag of loofahs.*

*Exit* **David,** *enter* **Jane.**

**Tom** Ready?

**Jane** What for?

**Tom** To actually *do* something, you great lump of entropy.

**Jane** Why me? Why not Brenda?

**Tom** Brenda doesn't like the police.

**Jane** Oh well then, that's alright. I love the police. I especially love them arresting me.

**Tom** Coming?

**Jane** Why should I?

**Tom** Do you think the systematic oppression of black people is a good thing.

**Jane** No. Of course not.

**Tom** And are you doing anything else of global importance this morning?

**Jane** No.

**Tom** Well then.

**Jane** If my father was alive he'd spin in his grave.

*They leave.*

**Brenda** *comes on with a bowl of cat food and a bowl of dog food. Puts them on the floor. Picks up a paper bag and takes out a new tub of fish food.*

**Brenda** (*reads*) Float some on top of the water, as much as your fishes like.

*Turns on TV.*

**Brenda** The fishes will eagerly devour it.

*Opening credits of Australian soap on TV.* **Brenda** *feeds the fish. The lights fade.*


Scene Four

*Lights up in the living room.*

*The TV is on.*

**Sam** *is sitting at the table. He has a death-mask on his face, in fact a plaster of Paris mould. Two straws stick out from under his nose.*

**David** *dashes in. His trousers are muddy from the knee down. He has been walking miles. He is exhausted, frustrated, and angry. Rushes to the phone. Hasn't got any change. Goes over to* **Sam.**

**David** Have you got any . . . Jesus Christ. What the hell are you doing?

*It looks at him.*

**David** Never mind.

*He runs upstairs.*

**Jane** *arrives through the front door.*

**Jane** Hello. Jesus Christ. What the hell are you doing?

*It looks at her.*

**Jane** You're Sam, aren't you? I'm Jane. Brenda! Is your mother in? Would she mind if I made a cup of tea? What are you doing?

**Sam** (*indistinct*) How can I answer you when I can't move my mouth?

**Jane** Sorry.

*She goes into the kitchen.*

**Sam** *taps the mask to see that it's set, then peels it off.* **David** *comes downstairs and screams outrageously at the face underneath.*

**Sam** Very funny.

**David** What are you doing?

**Sam** I'm making a video nasty.

**David** A what?

**Sam** Don't tell my mother. She'd go apeshit.

**David** I'm not surprised

*Goes to the phone and dials.*

**David** What's making a video nasty got to do with dipping your head in a bowl full of gunk?

**Sam** I'm making a head cast, what do you think? It's special effects, this.

**Jane** *returns.*

**Jane** That's an improvement. So, what are you doing?

**Sam** I'm making a head cast.

**Jane** Sounds disgusting.

**Sam** Well as a matter of fact, horror film technology has revolutionised medical prosthetics.

**Jane** Prosthetics?

**Sam** Rubber bits.

**Jane** This is a hobby, is it?

**Sam** Yes. The last one I made was hopeless. The first one I made someone sat on.

*He points to the head that* **Jane** *encountered previously.*

**Sam** Hardly lifelike at all. I'm getting better.

**Jane** And what's the end result?

**Sam** A video nasty. Sex and violence.

**Jane** Sex as well?

**Sam** Yeh. I do know about sex.

**Jane** I'm sure you do.

**Sam** But I can't find a girl that knows how to scream properly. Plenty of blokes at school know how to push them down and get on top of them but I can't find a good screamer. They all keep on giggling. I can't stand girls. Don't tell my mother. She hates the things I like.

**Jane** I can't imagine why.

*Kettle whistles,* **Jane** *exits.*

**David** Hello, Tish? David Sinclair. Am I on a job this afternoon? / Talk to Bob, why? / Well, I'm in, um Cornwall, why? / Bob! Hi Bob. / I'm in um, Cornwall. / Look I filed a hundred words, have . . . / You got them? Good. / What? / What? / Jesus. Bob, I'm having trouble hearing you. This is a very bad line. Can I call you back? / I'll call you back.

*Puts phone down.*

**David** Jesus H. Christ.

*Dials again.*

**Jane** *returns with tea.*

**Jane** They arrested Tom.

**Sam** Again?

**Jane** Should we do anything?

**Sam** Nope.

**Jane** He sat in the doorway of Sainsbury's and yelled for an hour.

**Sam** Didn't the police stop him?

**Jane** Well, they arrived soon enough, but they couldn't move him.

**Sam** Why not.

**Jane** He was covered in red paint. Gloss.

*So are her hands.*

**Jane** Finally the police tried to lift him on to a blanket, but every time they began to lift, he started screaming that he had very brittle bones, a delicate skull, and a black belt in Tai Kwon Do. He's completely shameless.

**Sam** He's completely stupid. Everyone who comes here's bonkers.

**Jane** I've something to show you.

*She goes upstairs.*

**David** Andrew? You stupid bastard. / Grateful? You phone in a story . . . my story . . . and you're not even bloody well there. / That's not the point. You should have waited for the P.A report, that's the point. / I agree. It's a very simple story. Prime Minister opens ring road. Not much scope for inaccuracy. Unless of course she doesn't actually fucking open the God damn fucking ring road. She's in hospital, you dickhead, detached her bloody retina. Jesus, Andrew, I mean . . . don't you even listen to the news? / Look, next time I want a favour, do me a favour and don't do it.

*Puts phone down.* **David** *dials again.*

**Sam** Would you like to be in my film?

**David** I don't think so.

**Sam** You could have your eye poked out with a rivet gun.

**David** I'll pass, thanks.

**Sam** Or a stabbing? I've got a proper knife.

**David** Bob? / What can I say, Bob? / Yes, I got the story phoned in and it was the wrong bloody story and I'm very sorry . . . / Look, Bob, ask yourself why. Why would I fuck you up over this? / I know you did, but . . . Look, I was not pissed. / Well, you can talk. / That's as maybe, but this is a good story. / What? / Well no, not yet. / Bob, you don't hire and fire, so don't make idle threats; Peter's the one who hires and fires, Bob? . . . / Hi Peter. / Yes. / No, of course not. / What? / Oh come on, Peter, you don't mean that. Don't let Bob wind you up. Peter . . . Peter? Oh shit.

*He puts the phone down.*

**Sam** You shouldn't swear in front of me. I'm very impressionable.

**David** *opens a bottle of Scotch and swigs.*

**Sam** Have you seen 'The Evil Dead?'

**David** I used to work for them.

**Sam** *leaps up and puts a video tape on.* **Jane** *returns with the photo of* **David** *and questions* **Sam** *as he prepares the video.*

**Jane** Have you ever seen this man? Sam? Answer me.

**Sam** You mean David?

**Jane** You know him? He was here?

**Sam** Of course he was.

**Jane** Oh thank God, and thank you, Sam.

**Sam** Can you scream?

**Jane** What happened to him?

**Sam** You could be my leading lady if you can scream. Watch.

**Sam** *runs the video. They watch a decapitation.*

**David** That's disgusting.

**Jane** Lovely. Sam, answer me.

**David** How do they do that?

**Sam** He was here. Then he left.

**David** Invisible edit?

**Jane** Did he say where he was going? Please, Sam. I need to know.

**Brenda** *comes in with shopping.*

*Video off.*

**Brenda** Here we are then.

**Sam** Oh shit.

*He tries to tidy up.*

**Brenda** Oh, Sam. Look at the mess. And this horrible thing. I wish you'd grow up and out of all this. They said you would. When will you?

**Sam** It's just a hobby, that's all.

**Brenda** Do it in the shed then, where no one can see you.

**Sam** *goes out through the kitchen.*

**Brenda** I don't go in Sam's shed. It's horrible in Sam's shed. Thought I'd put a stop to this.

**Jane** It's hard to know where they get it from, isn't it? All this sex and violence.

**Brenda** Not from no one. Not from anywhere, not Sam.

**Jane** The TV probably.

**Brenda** No. He makes it up. It's all in his head. But that's alright. That's perfectly normal. Behaviour, that's all it is.

**Jane** Tea in the pot.

**Brenda** Lovely.

**Brenda** *leaves to get some.*

**Jane** *sits on the sofa,* **David** *rising just before she settles.*

**David** *goes upstairs. As he gets to the top* **Sam** *suddenly appears in front of him, screaming. He repeatedly plunges a knife into* **David**'s *chest.*

**David** Jesus Christ. Fuck off.

**Sam** Were you frightened?

**David** I'll break your bloody neck for you.

*Enter* **Brenda** *with shopping.*

**Brenda** Here we are then. What's going on?

**David** Your son's a bloody lunatic.

**Sam** *stabs himself repeatedly, dies.*

**Brenda** Did you give him Smarties?

**David** If I was his father I'd give him a bloody good hiding.

**Brenda** They go funny on Smarties.

**David** Where is his father anyway?

**Brenda** Nowhere.

**Sam** Dead.

**Brenda** Not dead. Gone away, that's all.

**Sam** He's dead, or he'd come and see me. I reckon he's dead anyway. Don't sit down!

**David** *sits on* **Sam***'s mask.*

**David** Oh sod it.

**Sam** You cracked it, you f . . . idiot!

**Sam** *leaves.*

**Brenda** Don't mind Sam. He's a good boy.

**David** Is Tom back yet?

**Brenda** Usually in the pub at lunchtime.

**Brenda** *goes into the kitchen.* **David** *drinks, then goes the same way as* **Sam***. Pauses at the door, opens it very cautiously. As he relaxes and disappears,* **Jane** *jumps up from the sofa with a scream.*

**Brenda** (*off*) What's that?

**Jane** Something furry.

**Brenda** Happy hamster. Sam's always leaving him out.

**Brenda** *enters with tray.*

**Brenda** Did you catch him?

**Jane** I didn't try.

**Brenda** Oh well, he'll pop out again.

**Jane** *fingers the Encylopaedias.*

**Jane** Whose are these?

**Brenda** Oh. *Encyclopaedia Britannica.*

**Jane** Are they yours?

**Brenda** Fell off the back of a lorry.

**Jane** Do you use them at all?

**Brenda** No, never. I'd love to be bright but I'm thick. That thick I've no idea. There's one thing I do know mind you, that hardly no one else does. I know what a cephalic index is. I opened one of them. Just after they'd come one night I settled down and took one on my lap and opened it and I learned cephalic index. I don't remember nowt else, because I thought to remember cephalic index I'd better close the book to remember, then the phone, I forget . . . except the smell. Do you know what a cephalic index is?

**Jane** No.

**Brenda** No. No one does. No one ever has. But you know what's surprising? What's surprising is the number of times you can bring it up in conversation when you do know what it means. They smell lovely if you open them. But where to start? There's yards of it. But that's nice. It's nice to have it all in one. Knowledge. It's nice to know that there it all is. If there were the time.

**Jane** (*reading*) How wide your skull is, as compared to how long.

**Brenda** (*smiles*) Cephalic index. I talk to you. That's a turn up.

**Jane** Brenda, Sam said he recognised David.

**Brenda** No.

**Jane** He was very sure. He even said he liked him. That means you've been lying to me.

**Brenda** No.

**Jane** Brenda, I'm not cross, but I want to know why you're lying. Did something happen to him?

**Brenda** What do you mean?

**Jane** An illness, an accident, God knows.

**Brenda** No.

**Jane** I hope not.

**Brenda** No accidents around here. No pain, no nothing. No violence.

**Tom** *enters behind them, covered in red paint.*

**Tom** Hello.

**Jane** Jesus.

**Brenda** Oh, Tom!

**Tom** It's alright, Brenda, it's paint. It's only paint.

**Brenda** Oh look at you, Tom. Look at you. Look at him. He's out of his box, isn't he, Jane? You're out of your box you are.

**Tom** I am. And they're not going to get me back in.

**Brenda** Something wrong with his cephalic index.

**Jane** Just what I was going to say.

**Brenda** You ought to be locked up.

**Tom** I was.

**Jane** What are you out on, bail?

**Tom** No, I'm out because I can only use a Thompson-Kearney Facility Lavatory, so I demanded a Thompson-Kearney Facility Lavatory and they didn't have one, so they let me out.

**Jane** What *is* a Thompson-Kearney Facility Lavatory?

**Tom** Christ knows.

**Brenda** You need a bath.

**Tom** True.

**Brenda** I'll get the turps.

*She goes.*

**Jane** Did they hurt you?

**Tom** No. Surprisingly sensitive, the Cumbrian police. Did they bother you?

**Jane** No, I ran. I went to the pub. The pub round the corner.

**Tom** Oh?

**Jane** The manager recognised David's photo. Said he'd been in a couple of times. With you.

**Brenda** *returns with the turps. She begins to clean* **Tom** *down, starting with his hands.*

**Jane** Well?

**Tom** Well what?

**Jane** Why all this secrecy?

**Tom** I don't like talking to strangers. I got drunk once with a very attractive woman. Next day some friends of mine tried to put to sea and their dinghy sank. She was Special Branch.

**Jane** Well I'm not bloody Special Branch. And they don't waste their time investigating idiots who pour paint over themselves.

**Tom** They do if it's red paint.

**Jane** You're a political fanatic.

**Tom** And you're a political invention. Articulate, attractive female, non-rad Lib-fem, urban model, circa 1990.

**Jane** All I want is my husband!

**Tom** And eleven other endearing phrases. Just pull cord and release.

**Jane** What were you two involved in? A writer and a radical, a few miles from Sellafield. Have you been told to keep quiet? Did he find out something he wasn't meant to know?

**Tom** Look out!

**Jane** What?

**Tom** Flying pig.

**Brenda** Where?

**Jane** Answer me.

**Tom** There's nothing to know about Sellafield. No secrets; it's just an old irradiated nuclear plant with big cracks in it. It's killed every fish from here to Wales and it may well kill us all. It's a serious issue, not a red herring in this domestic murder mystery of yours.

**Jane** Who said anything about murder?

**Tom** You did.

**Jane** No I didn't.

**Tom** Shh!

**Jane** What?

**Tom** Speak quietly.

**Jane** Why?

**Tom** Brenda might be wired for sound.

**Brenda** Tom, keep still.

**Tom** Testing, testing . . .

**Brenda** Tom!

**Jane** You said murder.

**Tom** I was referring to the events taking place in your head. You're deliberately avoiding the simplest explanation.

**Jane** Which is?

**Tom** He's left you.

**Jane** No.

**Tom** Took off one morning and didn't come back.

**Jane** He wouldn't do that.

**Tom** Maybe he doesn't want to be found.

*Pause.*

**Jane** Was he with another woman? Is that what this is all about? It is, isn't it? Brenda?

**Brenda** Mmm?

**Tom** Get me to the bathroom eh, Brenda?

**Brenda** Right.

**Jane** He *was* here. So tell me what happened.

**Tom** That's not up to me.

**Brenda** *wheels* **Tom**, *stops.*

**Brenda** He did stay.

**Tom** Brenda.

**Brenda** It's alright, Tom. He was on his own. He stayed a couple of days, then he left. That's all. We don't know where, do we, Tom?

**Tom** No. But you're right, Jane. He did discover something nasty up here. It was wearing his shoes.

**Brenda** *wheels him out.*

**Jane** *considers following them, but instead grabs her coat and leaves.*

**David** *comes in. He has been drinking steadily.*

**David** Tom! Tom!

**Tom** *emerges, miraculously clean.*

**Tom** Greetings, snoop.

**David** What can I say, Tom? Thank you. I phoned in the story. They held the front page. And rewrote the leader. Half page picture, splash headline: 'Power Protest Prospers'. Two columns, eight-point bold: 'The security of our nation's nuclear installations was severely tested today when a mad dwarf on wheels waggled a loofah at visitors to the Sellafield Exhibition Centre. The protest continued for all of two and a half minutes, by which time police hero Constable Plod had found the brake on the wheelchair and bravely pushed the lone protester into a bush. A government spokesman said we will never give in to terrorism or any brand of toiletry.'

**Tom** The trouble with sarcasm, David, is that eventually it replaces everything else.

**David** I've got nothing else now, you pathetic bastard. Except pneumonia. I've travelled two hundred miles, ruined a very good pair of shoes, and lost my bloody job! All for that futile little stunt.

**Tom** If you refuse to report it, yes of course it's futile.

**David** Where were the others? Where were the students in skeleton leotards and gasmasks? Where were the old ladies with snapshots of their grandchildren? Where were the lesbians? Where was Tony Benn?

**Tom** Everybody round here works for BNF.

**David** Then why bother?

**Tom** Somebody has to.

**David** Somebody. Your body?

**Tom** I'll have you know that two and a half million spermatazoa underwent a mammoth trial of strength and endurance to produce me.

**David** Well, God knows how yours won.

**Tom** Must have had a head start.

**David** Must have had a speedboat. Or maybe the others let him win. Maybe they had a policy of positive discrimination.

**Tom** I know I'm only one small voice. That's why I need you to amplify it.

**David** Well, you've nobbled the wrong horse. I needed a fucking good story, not a duckling on a dog's head. I've lost my job!

**Tom** You're a big disappointment to me.

**David** Well God, Tom, I'm so sorry.

**Tom** You're not what I expected. I expected a crusader. Someone who believed in something.

**David** A salary, that's what I believed in.

**Tom** Don't be facetious. You don't believe in anything.

**David** Well frankly, no. No, I don't.

**Tom** Why not?

**David** Time of life.

**Tom** What happened in your life to make it so deadly?

**David** That's none of your fucking business.

**David** *kicks the globe. Catches it. Staggers out.*

*Lights fade.*


Scene Five

*Lights up on the beach.*

**Jane** *sits watching the ocean.* **Buddy** *enters behind her.*

**Buddy** Hi.

**Jane** Ha!

**Buddy** I'm sorry.

**Jane** Christ. Sorry.

**Buddy** I made you jump.

**Jane** No, I'm just a bit jumpy.

**Buddy** I'm Buddy.

**Jane** I'm Jane.

**Buddy** Welcome to the beach, Jane.

**Jane** I saw you here this morning. And yesterday as I arrived. In fact every time I pass the beach, you're here.

**Buddy** And you're here too.

**Jane** I'm just passing through. You're always here. One person on the whole beach and when you get closer it's always you.

**Buddy** I like the beach. The tide here is very dramatic. It goes out a long way. You're not from around here, are you?

**Jane** Well, neither are you.

**Buddy** No, but I belong. Why are you here?

**Jane** I'm looking for a man. His name's David. He's disappeared.

*She hands* **Buddy** *the photograph.*

**Jane** Do you know him at all?

**Buddy** Shh.

**Jane** What?

**Buddy** Feel that?

**Jane** Feel what?

**Buddy** The tide's turning.

**Jane** You never saw him?

**Buddy** If you keep still enough you can feel the wave that turns the tide. We are 78 per cent water. We turn with it.

**Jane** The earth turns and the tide comes in. I can understand that. But it goes back out again.

**Buddy** Mmmhmm?

**Jane** Why doesn't it just keep on coming?

**Buddy** It's not the earth.

**Jane** What isn't?

**Buddy** It's the moon. If the earth was independent of the moon, then yes, the tide would drown us all.

**David** *enters, dribbling the plastic globe. His trousers are in a worse state. He carries a whisky bottle. He is very drunk.*

**Buddy** What sort of a man was your husband?

**Jane** Well, he was . . . Um . . .

**David** Fuck them all.

**Jane** He was a nice man.

**David** Shit heads. As Sinclair takes it down the wing.

**Jane** Articulate. Patient. Gentle.

**David** *boots the globe.*

**David** And it's there! Fuck them all. Sinclair! England! Sinclair!
England!

**Jane** A very English man, really. Not as in typically English,
as in . . . English, you know.

**Buddy** But what sort of man was he?

**Jane** He was . . . my husband. He was a nice man. He was
a bit . . .

**Buddy** What?

**Jane** Well, like everyone else nowadays. You know.

**Buddy** Depressed or dangerous?

**Jane** No. No. He was a good man. Honest and upright.

**David** *falls over.*

**Buddy** Did he drink?

**Jane** No. Well, a bit. Not much.

**Buddy** He sounds almost perfect.

**Jane** Yes.

*Pause.*

**Jane** Well, nobody's that. He was a bit . . .

**Buddy** What?

**Jane** Nothing.

**Buddy** A bit what?

**Jane** Immersed.

**Buddy** Immersed?

**Jane** I loved him very much.

**Buddy** Immersed in what?

**Jane** Himself.

**Buddy** Ah.

**Jane** Like a lot of intelligent people.

**Jane** *looks out to sea.*

**David** *is now the one on the beach with* **Buddy**.

**David** The people are stupid. What's your name, friend?

**Buddy** Buddy.

**David** What's your name, buddy?

**Buddy** That's my name.

**David** American?

**Buddy** Once upon a time.

**David** What was I talking about?

**Buddy** The British.

**David** That's right. This is what I have learned in my thirty-odd years about the British people. I mean the mass of them. The Great British mass. Is fundamentally and irrevocably stupid. 70 million of them without an original thought in their heads. I have spent my life attempting to raise the consciousness of this mass. I have implored and encouraged. I have used words of few syllables. I have attempted to communicate about the state of the world in the hope that the mass might begin to change it. 3 million of the dozy sods read me. In 3 million ears and out the other 3 million. Another 3 million of them don't read anything at all.

And another 3 million, did you know this? Can't read! Don't be fooled by the people you rub shoulders with in wine bars and with whom you ardently discuss the dismantling of the Welfare State and what's coming down from Stratford. Don't be fooled into forgetting that most of the country is talking and thinking about Linda Lusardi's tits and another honest copper murdered by another gang of black rapists. Don't be fooled into believing the country is actually populated by people who can actually think!

**Jane** He was a thinker.

**David** Drink?

**Jane** I used to think he thank . . .

**Buddy** I think you're drunk.

**Jane** . . . thunk?

**David** I think so too.

**Jane** Too much for his own good.

**David** We drinkers, I mean thinkers, are in a minority of a majority so overwhelming in their mental simplicity, in their dull thick-headedness that our own tiny spark of intellectual capacity would be swamped and extinguished by them in an instant if it were not for the vile gas of privilege and dare I say it? superiority, that helps us keep rising to the top, like the creamy farts we are.

**Jane** He was a socialist. When I met him. Full of hate for his father; aimed it all at everything his father stood for, and my family too as a matter of fact. I'm a bit of a lost cause actually, marrying him. I'll be sorry, but I'm not.

**David** It's the premise that all men are equal that dangles our balls in the Tory vice. It's patently obvious that all men are not equal. I mean, you may well be a better . . . beach bum than I am. I am not equal to you in the accomplishments of beach bummery perhaps. And I can't drive a wheelchair like

Tom. And if our personal wheelcount or our collections of flotsam and jetsam were a measure of success and happiness in this world, then you might be both of you, top of the heap. However. But. Ultimately. A knowledge of these things is not worth two good arms and two good legs and money in the bank. Equality is a false premise. Teach them what you like; some brains remain bigger than others. And some women have archetypal playground bodies and others I personally wouldn't touch with a ten-foot pole. The point about life is, and this is the point; it isn't fair. It isn't even women and children first. It's every man for himself.

**Jane** He was a very happy man. When we met. But something died inside him, and all his words were rotting.

**Buddy** You believe in the inequality of man?

**David** I believe in life as it is lived.

**Buddy** But life is lived appallingly. Inequality is not a fundamental truth. It's a by-product of defining ourselves. Somewhere along the line, God forgive us, we decided to be tall, white, male and rich, and to hell with Them.

**David** Three out of four. Will I go to heaven?

**Jane** It was hope, it was his hope that died.

**Buddy** What do you do for a living?

**David** I am a small cog in a large machine that tells people what to think.

**Jane** He was a writer.

**David** The machine is a liar, of course.

**Jane** A good writer, too.

**David** And whichever way it turns, the smallest cog is as guilty as the mainspring. I think I'll drown myself.

**Buddy** Sit right where you are and you will.

*A wave laps* **Jane***'s feet.*

**Jane** Arrgh!

**Buddy** You gotta watch the sneaky little ones there.

**Jane** Thanks for the warning.

**David** *gives the globe to* **Buddy.**

**David** Here.

**Buddy** Thank you. Don't you want it?

**David** I don't know what the fuck to do with it!

**David** *staggers off.*

**Jane** When I was a kid I'd try to pick a wave way out in the distance; the wave that would grow and grow and just keep growing I suppose, and drown us all. All my waves were disappointments. Have you been here long? In England?

**Buddy** A while.

**Jane** Where did you come from?

**Buddy** Montana, via the moon.

**Jane** Uh huh. And before you stood on the beach all day, what did you do?

**Buddy** I worked for NASA. I was an Apollo astronaut.

**Jane** A what?

**Buddy** An astronaut. Somebody had to be.

**Jane** What's your name?

**Buddy** I'm the one whose name no one can remember.

**Jane** *gives a laugh, stifles it. Looks at him. He is entranced, open. He is mad as a hatter, or telling the truth.*

**Jane** How was the moon?

**Buddy** Very fine. Still feel the pull.

**Jane** I have to go now. It's getting dark.

*She walks away.*

**Buddy** Here.

*Throws her the globe.*

**Jane** What for?

**Buddy** You'll think of something.

**Jane** *goes cautiously.*

**Buddy** It was not my help they wanted, nor each other's. I guessed they were going through a separation not so much from each other as from the selves they had once loved. A journey of the soul is measured not with maps and compass points but with meetings, and encounters not with fellow travellers, but with those you pass. They are there to teach you a little of the landscape they know better. David's journey was to be the most treacherous, especially as he returned home that evening to Brenda's house. Because at Brenda's house that evening, he was to meet the Devil.

*Lights Fade.*

# Act Two

Scene One

*Night.* **Jane** *returns home from the beach. The house is empty, deathly quiet. The room is quite dark, but the stairwell is lit. A video camera on a tripod points towards the stairwell.*

*The* **Parrot** *gives a low rumbling squawk.*

**Jane** Just say it will you? Even if you don't mean it.

*She strokes the* **Parrot**. *It bites her finger.*

**Jane** Ow!

*A bump from upstairs.*

**Jane** *investigates, cautiously.*

**Jane** Sam?

*The head comes bouncing down the stairs and lands at her feet. She picks it up.*

**Jane** Very funny, Sam. But once is enough.

*Getting no reply, she turns away from the foot of the stairs.*

**Sam** *springs up from behind the sofa.* **Jane** *screams.*

**Jane** You sod.

**Sam** Fishing line, see? Simple.

**Sam** *detaches the video camera from its tripod.*

**Jane** Am I on that?

**Sam** Do you mind?

**Jane** Yes.

**Sam** I have to work at night. Avoid my mother.

**Jane** Sam, how long was David here?

**Sam** Who?

**Jane** Don't start. David.

**Sam** Oh, him.

**Jane** Where did he go?

**Sam** Will you give me a hand?

**Jane** Sam. Did he tell you where he was going?

**Sam** Maybe. Help me first.

**Jane** Two minutes.

**Sam** Brilliant. This bloke's head gets chopped off at the top of the stairs, right? I can't shoot that bit yet. Then it rolls to the bottom, right?

*He hands her the head.*

**Sam** Hold that.

**Jane** Is this paint?

**Sam** No.

**Jane** Good.

**Sam** It's pig's blood.

**Jane** Oh God.

**Sam** Just stand halfway up the stairs and when I say 'action', roll it down.

**Jane** Why is there a worm instead of an eye?

**Sam** The worm popped his eye out.

**Jane** Ask a silly question.

**Sam** It's a worm lives inside me and when I whisper in your ear or kiss you or anything, you've had it because the worm crawls in. It's a very long worm and it pierces your eardrum and slides around inside your nasal passage and pops your eyes out from behind. You can grab it then if you're quick, and pull it out through your eye socket like a tapeworm. Or if you're in a lot of pain you just give up and decapitate yourself. Alright, standby.

**Jane** What about the mess?

**Sam** Action!

*She drops the head.* **Sam** *shoots, handheld.*

**Jane** Now tell me about David.

**Sam** Could you aim more for the banisters?

**Jane** Sam!

**Sam** *hands her back the head.*

**Sam** He was alright, David. He was quite useful for a while.

**Jane** How?

**Sam** Don't you recognise him?

*She drops the head.*

**Jane** Jesus.

**David** *enters with a hard white mask on. One eye hole.*

**David** (*distinct*) When the hell can I take this off?

**Sam** Soon. Careful.

**Sam** *leads* **David** *to the sofa and sits him down.*

**Sam** The harder it grows the more brittle it gets, so don't move your face.

**David** How the bloody hell could I move my face?

**Sam** He let me plaster of Paris him. Nobody else would.

**Jane** And then?

**Sam** He left.

**Jane** In one piece? Or did you dismember him first?

**Sam** Don't be ridiculous. It's only latex.

**David** Aaargh!

*He leaps up from the sofa and turns in a circle. Happy hamster has paid another visit to the outside world.*

**Sam** David!

**David** What the fuck was that?

**Sam** Keep still. What's the matter?

**David** A rat. There's a rat in the sofa.

**Sam** A what?

**David** A rat.

**Sam** Not a rat, it's a hamster that's all. Stop moving about. Sit down.

**David** Have you got it?

**Sam** God, hold on.

**Sam** *plunges his arm down the back of the sofa. Fails to find the hamster, but brings up a dusty video cassette, which he blows the fluff off and leaves on the arm of the sofa.*

**Sam** Alright, got it. You can sit down now.

**David** You got it.

**Sam** Want to feel?

**David** No.

**Sam** *rattles a cage, pretending to put the hamster in.*

**David** Right.

**David** *sits.*

**Jane** His nose is wonky.

**Sam** His nose was wonky.

**Jane** His face is too fat. Bloated. As if he'd drowned.

*Enter* **Tom**.

**Tom** Sam.

**Sam** Shit.

**Tom** Now what in hell do you think you're doing?

**Sam** She's asleep.

**Tom** That is no excuse.

**Sam** I'll clean up the mess.

**Tom** You made the mess, Sam, that's what I'm objecting to. (*To* **Jane**.) And what are you? A Welsh scrum half? Get it cleaned up, Sam. Before you give your mother a coronary.

**Sam** Oh, Tom.

**Tom** Do as you're told. It's a wild goose chase anyway, Sam. How are you going to edit this epic? Scissors and sellotape?

**Sam** You're not my father.

*Exit* **Sam**.

**David** Sam. This is very boring. Sam.

**David** *finds the video tape under his hand.*

**Jane** I'm sorry, I sort of encouraged him.

**Tom** Sam has certain morbid interests it would be best to discourage.

**Jane** Perfectly normal isn't it? Kids and sex and violence. One day it's postman's knock and the next it's murder in the dark.

**Tom** Go to bed.

**Jane** As soon as you've told me where he went.

**Tom** We don't know.

**Jane** How am I supposed to believe that when you lied about knowing him, you lied about his being here . . .

**Tom** *turns to go.*

**Jane** I'm not leaving.

**Tom** There are things it's not my place to tell you.

**Jane** Well, they're the things I need to know. Aren't they?

**Tom** *leaves.* **Jane** *throws the head at his closed door.*

**David** *has managed to get a video into the machine and has sat himself in front of the telly. Using the remote control, he switches on.*

**Jane** *goes upstairs.*

*On the TV, a few seconds of 'Life on Earth' about whales.*

*Bad video edit (hiss and colour-buzz); short burst of soap credits.*

*Bad video edit, short burst of BBC sex drama.*

*Bad video edit and into old home video. Cheap end of the market colours. A young* **Sam** *fools around for the camera.*

*Bad video edit into static shot. The camera pointed at a sofa. For a moment the sofa remains empty and then* **Michael** *enters the frame, and sits in big close up.*

**Michael** *is bearded, and has a slight stammer. A nervous twisting of the neck. Quiet torment beneath a sad exterior.*

**Michael** Um. I can't say I'm sorry. Not that I'm not. But . . . I think I understand something now. Part of it. Last night I, um . . . That's um . . . I were in her bedroom she had a single bed with a plastic top with brass pins and candlewick. I'd done it to her. I were still doing it. She were gone, but I were making it worse.

**David** *peels his mask off.*

What's the point in being sorry? I'd been needing to make it worse and worse, which I never could understand. Something . . . There was a wardrobe door swung open and shoes fell out. Earlier. In the door was a mirror. I reached round for my Phillips' I think and I saw my foot in the mirror. My foot and hers in the mirror, for real. I could see it for real, my foot and hers. I dragged her down the bed 'til I could see her in the mirror. And me, in the mirror, and I finished, watching in the mirror . . .

**Brenda** *appears and stares in horror at the television. Shocked to the bone.*

**Brenda** No!

*She rushes to the sofa, finds the remote control. Freeze frames the picture.*

**David** You're Brenda. Jesus.

**Brenda** *is mesmerised by the silent picture long enough for* **David** *to take the remote from her. He starts the tape again and Brenda collapses, her hands to her ears.*

**Michael** And when I were finished I was finished. Satisfied, like I'd never been. Inside. Watching in the mirror, see, it's somehow made it real. And I felt good. And tonight, I'd just started on another and it was so real I didn't have to. And I stopped. I think it might be over now. I'm sorry.

*Static.*

**David** *turns to look at* **Brenda**.

**Brenda** When they'd taken him they took me upstairs and showed me his box. Said when did I know. Said I never knew. Opened his box. Made me look in. Said recognise that? Said no. Screwdriver. I didn't recognise nothing. I didn't know nothing. Said pull the other one, one of them. But no, I never knew.

**David** You're Brenda.

**Brenda** And Sophie doesn't know. And Sam was far too young. It's not even in the past for them. It never was, and mustn't be.

**David** That was Michael Armstrong, wasn't it? And you're Brenda.

**Brenda** And no one round here, neither.

**David** You're a legend, do you know that? Not one statement, not one photograph, no one on the Street managed to track you down, not before the trial, not during the trial, and not after the trial. You're a legend.

**Brenda** I'm just me, please.

**David** It was that bloody priest. Nobody could get further than that bloody priest.

**Brenda** He was kind. I never even went to church. But he did it all for me. Sold the house in Gosforth. This place was cheaper. Had some left over. Run out now.

**David** Can I have this?

**Brenda** No!

**David** Do you realise what it's worth?

**Brenda** No. Where did it come from?

**David** Do you realise how much money you could make?

**Brenda** No, please. Leave us alone.

*She takes the tape.*

**David** Brenda, trust me. I'm not some tabloid hack, I'm a serious . . . Brenda!

*She runs upstairs.*

**David** *thinks for a moment, then picks up the phone and dials.*

**David** Bob? It's David. / Yes I know it is but I thought you might like to know how the story turned out. / You're going to care, you are, because it's immense. / It's completely exclusive and it's gold dust. Unfortunately for you I'm not on salary so it's going to cost the paper an arm and a leg. / Because Bob, if you won't others will, believe me. With a story like this I can go to anyone I like. / Fine. If that's the way you feel. But Bob . . . don't you think you should have a quick word with Peter before I do? Just in case? / (*Smiles.*) I think you're being very sensible, Bob. I'll call you tomorrow. Or on the other hand, I might not.

*Puts phone down.*

**David** Thank you, God.

*Lights fade.*

Scene Two

*Someone moves around the darkened room.*

**Tom**'s *door opens and a shaft of light reveals* **Brenda**.

**Tom** (off) Brenda?

**Brenda** Tom.

**Tom** It's three o'clock in the morning. What are you doing?

**Brenda** I'm checking the animals, Tom.

**Tom** The animals are fine.

**Brenda** Are they alright, Tom?

**Tom** They all survived.

**Brenda** Because I dream of carnage now.

**Tom** Nasty word, Brenda.

**Brenda** Nasty dreams, Tom. Those gerbils, drowning in that mucky green aquarium. Neon tetras flopping on the floor of the mouse's cage. Budgie flapping up against the wires because its cage has got the cat in it.

**Tom** It's alright now, Brenda. You're safe, the kids are safe, the animals are safe.

**Brenda** In these dreams it always bursts and that aquarium holds a houseful of water. Drowns us skin and bones and fur and feathers. Lumps of catfood floating past the TV, floating. Cop shoots the darkie bobbing up and down past lovely old dog, gives up his doggy paddle didn't you? Goes under then.

**Tom** You'll not see him again.

**Brenda** My Mickey?

**Tom** Or David.

**Brenda** I never drown. Sometimes on the arm of the armchair, clinging on, claws out, waterlogged. Living room's an old canal by now. I'm a soaked and skinny old cat clinging on.

**Tom** *notices that she has a video tape in her hand.*

**Tom** Brenda?

**Brenda** And the aquarium floats by. The lights and the pump are still on; drying it out.

**Tom** Is that the tape?

**Brenda** Dry as a bone inside, it floats by. Fish lie on the rocks, drying out, curling up, last glimpse of all the water outside the glass. Little fossil house floating by with the furniture and the mothercare stuff and my comfortable shoes.

*He takes the tape from her.*

**Tom** Why don't we throw it away?

**Brenda** No.

**Tom** You don't want it.

**Brenda** Hide it, Tom.

**Tom** Alright.

**Brenda** Hide it well away, Tom, please.

**Tom** You should get to bed.

**Brenda** No. Staying down.

**Tom** Shall I make you some tea?

**Brenda** That'd be nice.

**Jane** *comes downstairs in her dressing gown.*

**Jane** I heard voices.

**Brenda** That was us. Me and Tom.

**Jane** Have you got an elastoplast? I can't stop bleeding.

**Tom** I'll get you one.

**Tom** *goes into the kitchen.*

**Jane** I think I owe you an apology. I'm not usually this paranoid. You say he just left; I've no reason not to believe you. I suppose I should just go home. I suppose.

**Brenda** I know. Home can be lonely. This sofa.

**Jane** Yes?

**Brenda** There's tears here, see. You can hardly see, but look. Cried them tears, so I know. Little tear stain. Look.

**Jane** *leans over to look closely.* **Brenda** *takes her bloodied finger and presses it on to the fabric.*

**Brenda** And blood. And . . . shh . . . look. Come. That's come, under there. Mickey's come, see?

**Jane** Who's Mickey?

**Tom** *returns.*

**Brenda** Got most of the paint off, didn't we, Tom?

**Jane** So I see.

**Tom** Except the important bits. They're still red.

**Jane** You mean your politics.

**Tom** I mean my bollocks. I've scoured everything else but my bollocks are sacred.

**Jane** *laughs, embarrassed.*

**Tom** Why don't you look at me?

**Jane** I am. I do. Don't I?

**Tom** Not as hard as you want to.

**Brenda** Go on, look at him.

**Jane** Alright, I'm looking.

**Tom** Look harder.

**Jane** I am looking. Really. Look, I'm looking.

**Tom** Harder.

*She looks very hard. Turns away embarrassed. Looks again. He raises his arm. She looks at it very closely. He smiles. She smiles.*

**Brenda** See?

**Jane** What's it like?

**Tom** What?

**Jane** Your life.

**Tom** It's like being trapped in a stop-action cartoon, like a plasticine man waiting for the animator to move you just enough for the next frame. If you move yourself, you fuck up the sequence, which pisses off the animator who pummels you into a lump again. Back behind the bars of who you are.

**Jane** But that's how I feel. That's how I've felt all my life.

**Tom** Here we are then. Both in the same canoe.

**Jane** Without a paddle.

**Tom** Or a canoe. Well, thank you. I was feeling a bit low but that's really cheered me up.

**Jane** I'm sorry.

**Brenda** Tom doesn't dwell.

**Tom** Ah, but I do. I shouldn't, but all creatures that on Earth do. Dwell.

**Jane** You're right, you shouldn't.

**Tom** You're right, I'm right. I really shouldn't. Let's go somewhere exciting with disabled access! Let's go to the library! Get them to break out the ramp. Let's go take a discreet piss behind the big wide door.

**Jane** I thought you campaigned for big wide doors and ramps.

**Tom** Yes. Into pubs, not fucking theatres. Into brothels and dogtracks, not the bloody town hall. (**Jane** *laughs*.) I make too many jokes. It's a dead giveaway. If jokes could kill I'd be a mass murderer.

**Jane** And are you?

**Tom** I thought we'd decided he was assassinated by the Central Electricity Generating Board.

**Jane** I know! I'm sorry.

**Tom** Do we look like murderers?

**Jane** It's not you I'm scared of, it's finding him. Being in a room I know he's been in that I've never been in with him, it's as if I made him up. All I've got is this memory of someone I loved but haven't yet met. If I don't find him soon he'll be a stranger. Did you get to know him?

**Tom** Eventually.

**Jane** How was he?

**Tom** Alive.

**Jane** He'd not been coming home. Not making love. Not loving me. That's all. Didn't love me. Anyone. And it made him furious, inside.

**Brenda** That look on his face.

**Jane** Did he tell you? Did he tell you what happened?

**Tom** Yes he did.

**Jane** What was it?

**Tom** You were there.

**Jane** But inside him? What happened?

**Brenda** Best not to know. I never.

**Brenda** *rises and swiftly climbs the stairs.* **David** *comes down them, she turns and tries to escape him, back into the living room.*

**David** Brenda? How would you like to earn ten thousand pounds?

**Brenda** What for?

**David** Some stories. Some memories. And the tape.

**Brenda** You mean in the papers?

**David** Yes.

**Brenda** (*very alarmed*) No!

**David** A serious article, maybe a short series.

**Brenda** No! No. I don't, I w . . . w . . . wouldn't w . . . w . . .

**David** Brenda, don't get excited. I'm just making you an offer.

**Brenda** No.

**David** Listen.

**Brenda** No!

**David** Listen!

**Brenda** I love my girl. I do. She's sunshine to me, my girl.

**David** Brenda, I understand . . .

**Brenda** You don't understand. Sophie and Sam don't know. Sophie and Sam mustn't know, because I know, and I know life's not worth living, it's not, if it wasn't for Sophie and Sam and not knowing.

**David** Others need to know.

**Brenda** I never knew.

**Tom** What happened between you two?

**Brenda** All I ever knew was . . .

**Jane** Nothing.

**Brenda** Him, that's all.

**Tom** Tell me.

**David** But how can we ever know? Our loved ones.

**Jane** Never.

**David** Or ourselves?

**Tom** Ever?

**Jane** No.

**Jane** *cuts herself off from* **Tom**.

**David** That's what I want to explore.

**Brenda** Tom!

**David** Shh. Brenda . . .

**Tom** *enters* **David***'s time scheme.*

**Tom** What? What's the matter?

**Brenda** He wants to tell, Tom. He wants to tell about my Mickey.

**David** Your words . . .

**Brenda** Tell him not to, Tom.

**David** The truth.

**Tom** Absolutely not, David.

**Brenda** I told you not to have him here.

**Tom** I'm sorry.

**David** Let's talk this through calmly. Let me tell you what I envisage.

**Tom** No.

**David** Before you dismiss it out of hand.

**Tom** Think what you're doing.

**David** Brenda will be fine.

**Tom** Brenda will not be fine.

**David** She'll make a lot of money.

**Tom** Christ, David. I can't for the life of me understand why Brenda's peace of mind is worth less to you than a few columns of filthy newsprint.

**David** Look, I'm a journalist. It's what I am.

**Tom** It's not all you are.

**David** I will not let compassion stand in my way here.

**Tom** You don't even like your job.

**David** I have to tell this story.

**Tom** Why?

**David** Because it's mine. I want to write about him. Whatever it was inside him.

**Brenda** Why?

**David** Because it happened.

**Brenda** Tom. That look on his face.

**Tom** Happened to whom?

**David** I could write a book. Forget the papers, I could write a book.

**Tom** Why this morbid fascination?

**David** Because it's part of us.

**Tom** What is?

**David** Whatever it was spilt from Brenda's husband! That sticky black darkness! It's in us all for Christ's sake, isn't it?

**Tom** All of us?

**David** Isn't it?

**Tom** In you, you mean?

*Pause.*

**David** Yes.

**Tom** Then maybe it's yourself you should be writing about.

*Pause.*

**Tom** Tell your own story.

**David** I don't have one.

**Tom** I don't believe you. If you want Brenda's story you might at least have the guts to tell your own.

*Pause.*

**David** It's a very short story.

**Tom** Tell us.

**David** She was . . .

**Tom** Yes?

**Jane** I was lying in the bath. This was the night before he left. We'd been arguing. About something. The bathroom floor I think. He left it wet. I dry it.

**David** I no longer love my wife, that's all.

**Jane** I was in the bath with my eyes closed. I heard him come in, I heard his electric shaver, then silence. I thought he must be looking at me. I hoped he was.

**David** It was as if she'd tied barbed wire round my heart. Nothing I did was right. Nothing I did was enough. Then there was a moment . . .

**Jane** His hand gripped my ankle, then he tugged and I went under. Opened my eyes, my mouth, and coughed what air I had up into my face and gone. I had no air until I'd struggled up on to my elbows, gasping, coughing . . . fire and water down my nose. Then he let go.

**David** I discovered that cold, black nugget in me. I stood over the bath. The cuff of my shirt was sopping wet.

**Jane** I prayed for him to smile. A smile to dilute the fear I felt. But for a second; who knows how long; no smile. Just surprise on his face and hate behind his eyes, hate that scampered back into his head to hide.

**David** The good boy that I am. The sensitive man. My intellect. My humour. My life. A sort of joke.

**Jane** Then he smiled. It was a joke.

**David** She thought it was a joke, the drowning.

**Both** But it wasn't.

**Jane** He'd meant it.

**David** We laughed it off.

**Jane** He left the room. I dried myself.

**David** Since then I've found it hard to care. About her, me, anyone. I have to know who Michael was, And why.

*He goes upstairs*

**Jane** I care what happened to him. I can't help but care. But I don't know why. I'm going for a walk.

**Jane** *leaves.*

*The sound of typing from upstairs.*

**Brenda** *hears it. It grows louder, more insistent, until it's an exaggerated death rattle of noise.*

**Brenda** Tom?

**Tom** It's alright, Brenda.

**Brenda** Make him stop, Tom. Make it not, Tom, shall I? It was all over. How can I make it all over again?

*Lights fade.*

Scene Three

*Moonlight up on the beach.* **Jane** *curled up, using the half inflated globe as a pillow.*

**Buddy** *arrives.*

**Buddy** Aren't you going to sleep in your bed?

**Jane** I'm sleeping here.

**Buddy** You'd better not.

**Jane** I'm sleeping right here.

**Buddy** Not if I were you.

**Jane** Well, you're not and I shall.

**Buddy** On the beach? At high tide?

**Jane** A really deep sleep. See that wave?

**Buddy** Down below the night tide?

**Jane** That wave there?

**Buddy** You wouldn't survive.

**Jane** That wave's mine.

**Buddy** Which one?

**Jane** The big one. It'll take us all.

*Pause.*

**Jane** Huh.

**Buddy** You'll have to wait a long time for the wave that doesn't break.

**Jane** If he's dead I wish I was. If he's somewhere nicer than dead, I still wish I was. And I wish he was.

**David** *appears on the beach, dressed to leave town. Thrusts a few typed pages at* **Buddy**.

**David** Buddy. Read this.

**Buddy** What is it?

**David** It's what I do.

**Buddy** *reads.* **David** *sits on his suitcase.*

*In the living room,* **Sam** *is asleep.* **Brenda** *brings the sleeping* **Sophie** *and lays her down to join him. Then she begins to stack the animal cages around the gas fire.*

**David** That's just the introduction. Can you imagine? That's the house. You'd never know. It's just a rough draft. What do you think?

**Buddy** What do you care?

**David** An opinion. It's an important story, don't you think?

**Buddy** How does it end?

**David** It doesn't end. Whatever pain gets passed around, life goes on, doesn't it?

**Brenda** *turns on the gas fire without lighting it. Settles down to die.*

**Buddy** How does she feel about it?

**David** Who?

**Buddy** This Brenda, who else?

**David** She's . . . concerned, naturally. She'll be OK. So what do you think?

**Buddy** I think it's very powerful.

**David** Absolutely. That's what I wanted to hear.

**Buddy** Tell me, are the English all so brim full of this obsessive despair?

**David** I've got a train to catch.

**Buddy** *nods.*

**Buddy** Do you like to swim?

**David** God no, I hate it. In fact I can't. As for the sea, it terrifies me. I never go near it.

**Buddy** Never?

**David** No.

**Buddy** Then how come you're so close to drowning?

**David** I'm not, am I?

**Buddy** *grabs him, trips him, holds his head under the water.*

**Buddy** Sure you are. You're way out of your depth, boy. Can you taste the salt? Can you feel the cold?

*Lets* **David** *up.*

**David** Jesus. You're out of your mind.

**Buddy** These are just the shallows.

**David** I could have drowned. I can't get on a train like this. I'll have to go back and change.

**Buddy** Good idea.

**David** *grabs his manuscript and suitcase and goes.*

**Buddy** (*shouts*) Ocean's all around you, boy, whether you like it or not. Only compassion will keep you afloat!

**Jane** You can murder me if you like, but don't fold me up and hide me in some awful cupboard.

**Buddy** You sound a little depressed.

**Jane** When I was a kid I used to eat cheese at bedtime for the nightmares. Maybe that's why I came. Maybe I need a murder mystery in my life.

**Buddy** There's no excuse for being depressed. You want not to be depressed?

**Jane** Yes, I want not to be depressed.

**Buddy** Then get back inside your body. Get your body back on earth and your head back on top of it.

**Jane** I don't understand you.

**Buddy** Depression is a schism between the body and the mind; the blood and the electric. You have to get back inside yourself. Go jump in the ocean. You will feel wet when you come out, you might feel damn cold, but you sure as hell won't feel depressed.

**Jane** I wouldn't be depressed if he still loved me.

**Buddy** (*deadly serious*) Don't delude yourself, girl. In matters of sadness and the ocean tides, and voyagers, I know a little more than you.

**Jane** Then help me.

**Buddy** Have a swim.

**Jane** Help me!

**Buddy** Hit the water. Tell the ocean hello.

*She considers it, changes her mind.*

**Jane** Don't be ridiculous.

**Buddy** Do it!

*She instantly walks into the ocean, towards the audience. Up to above her knees.*

**Jane** Oh Jesus.

**Buddy** Go on.

**Jane** I can't!

**Buddy** You've got a deep sadness.

**Jane** But my feet!

**Buddy** You need deep water.

**Jane** It's freezing.

**Buddy** It's October.

**Jane** Come with me.

**Buddy** What do you think I'm crazy?

**Jane** I knew it! You're a paddler.

**Buddy** Jane.

**Jane** I knew you were just a paddler!

**Buddy** You know you have to do this.

**Jane** All mouth and rolled up trousers.

**Buddy** Now or never and it's NOW!

**Jane** Oh G-o-d!

**Jane** *runs into the water, immersing herself.*

**Jane** Oh God it's cold it's cold it's cold it's so cold.

**Buddy** Do you feel alive?

**Jane** You'll have to define 'alive'.

**Buddy** That's not easy. Do you know how hard that is?
We flew a machine to Mars, do you remember, looking
for life beyond all this. A magic laboratory. But early on,
designing this Columbus, we realised we didn't know what

we were looking for. Is all life carbon-based? No idea. Could be unimaginable. Out hunting tigers, miss a field full of rabbits. They knew life on Mars would be dissimilar to life here, but *how* dissimilar?

**Jane** Jesus, there are fish in here.

**Buddy** How not to underestimate the dissimilarity? A man called Lovelock looked into it.

**Jane** Can I come out now?

**Buddy** No. He analysed all known life forms on earth. And he realised they all had one thing in common. They were all responsible for altering their environment.

**Jane** I wish I hadn't.

**Buddy** We eat, we excrete, we breathe in, we breathe out. A changing environment is evidence of life.

**Jane** Buddy, it's all a bit academic to me, considering I'm about to freeze to death.

**Buddy** Listen. Lovelock had this tremendous shock. He realised that this empirical evidence of life pertained not only to any living thing on earth, but also to the crew of an ocean-going liner, a farm, a theatre, a city. A road haulage firm, a family, a country, a continent. The *earth itself.*

**Jane** I'm coming out now.

**Buddy** Not yet! By complete accident, Lovelock had defined the world as a living organism.

**Jane** That's what I am.

**Buddy** It's as alive as you are.

**Jane** Buddy, I want to stay that way.

**Buddy** Beg Pardon?

**Jane** I want to stay that way. Can I come out now.

**Buddy** Of course you can.

*She wades out of the ocean.*

**Jane** Oh God. Now it's colder out. You know what I wish?

**Buddy** What?

**Jane** I wish I'd taken my clothes off.

**Buddy** Do you see what it all means?

**Jane** I am too wet to think. Too cold to care.

**Buddy** *grabs her.*

**Buddy** Never too cold to care, Jane. Never. If the earth is a living being then interdependance is no optional phenomenon. We *do* connect, and each of us have a personal responsibility to the whole. Now how do you feel?

**Jane** Well funnily enough, absolutely fantastic. I feel . . . crystal. I still don't believe I did this.

**Buddy** We can each be baptised into the new age or stay shipwrecked on the old one. Life sends out the strangest invitations.

**David** *appears in the house. He sniffs the air and registers what's going on.*

**David** Jesus.

**Buddy** Sometimes the choice is so simple, there is no choice.

**David** *runs to the window and throws it open. Turns off the gas.*

*He helps* **Brenda** *up. She's groggy, but quickly recovers.*

**David** *goes to pick up* **Sophie**, *but* **Brenda** *tries to stop him.*

**David** It's alright. I'm not going to hurt her. I'm not going to hurt her. I'm not going to hurt you. Here. Take her outside. Quickly.

**Brenda** *does as she's told.* **David** *picks up* **Sam***, who wakes and squirms a little.* **David** *carries him out.*

**Brenda** *returns.*

**Brenda** My animals.

**David** Alright! I'll save the animals. Get outside!

**David** *carries all the cages etc. out of the front door.*

*On the beach* **Jane** *is shivering.*

**Jane** Buddy, do you think I could remain true to the spirit of Aquarius if I wasn't soaking wet?

**Buddy** Mmm hmm?

**Jane** Because I have to get out of these things.

*She undresses. A moment of freezing embarrassment, then* **Buddy** *wraps his enormous coat around her. They settle.*

*First glimmer of dawn.*

**David** *and the family have left the house with two dogs, a cat, cages and a goldfish bowl.*

**Jane** What was it like being an astronaut, Buddy? What was it like on the moon?

**Buddy** Well, we went in search of what? Another life, new life forms. And there we were scuffing about in the darkness of the dust beneath our feet and found nothing and then I looked up and there it was. Life unrecognisable. It was up above us all the time. Here was a dead moon, but up there, the earth. A new life form, more complex than we'd ever imagined. All we had to do was live it.

**David** *and the family appear on another part of the beach.*

*In the distance, a ghostly glow from Sellafield.*

**Sam** *keeps his distance, tired but stoic.*

**David** She'll freeze. Here.

*Takes off his jacket for* **Sophie**.

**Brenda** Don't tell.

**David** I'm not going to tell. I promise.

**Brenda** Do you promise?

**David** Yes.

*He screws up his manuscript, tosses it.*

**Buddy** The earth exists now not beneath my feet but in my memory, and in my memory it is a jewel, a fluid crystal, the heart of a translucent, peaceful, and eminently wise creature. It beats for us. All we have to do is beat with it.

**Brenda** Used to be moonlight.

**David** Mmmhmm?

**Brenda** There used to be moonlight here. Can't feel the moonlight now, just the light from the 'lectric plant. My husband used to work there. His dad got him a job before he died. Leukaemia. He was in the papers. Not his name, but statistics. Mickey came home; he was late because the alarm went off on him and he had to shower twice. And the electric bill had come and we never had enough for that and then his mum came round and said his dad had died. And he wouldn't cry and sat there tight and looked at me and said, 'What are you crying for, you ugly cow, he was my dad.' 'God, you're an ugly cow,' he said, and then he went out. That night was the first one. I know what he did was wrong. But there's so much wrong about. That's killed children round here, and Michael's dad, and all those Russians, and that's not right. And the people round here, something in them's died living with all that. Living with all that, something's died in all of us.

**David** Hardly cause and effect though, Brenda.

**Brenda** What's that?

**David** The things you do . . . cause other things to happen.

**Brenda** Oh, no. I know. Just coincidence. But there's so much bad about now, it can't all be can it? Public and private. Good and bad's bigger than all that.

**Buddy** Lot of talk about destroying the earth. Heap of bullshit. We couldn't destroy it if we tried. All we could destroy is *ourselves*. And blow some dust the while into that great blue eye. And that great blue eye would blink and we'd be gone.

**Brenda** How do you feel?

**David** Alright. I feel good.

**Brenda** Good.

**Buddy** How do you feel?

**Jane** I don't know what to do.

**Buddy** Do what you feel.

**David** You know what it is? It's the head gets somehow separated . . .

**Jane** . . . Somehow separated from the heart.

**David** Doesn't it?

**Jane** *kisses* **Buddy**.

**Jane** I don't want to do that again.

**Buddy** That's alright, neither do I.

*They smile.*

**Buddy** I'd like to give you this.

**Jane** What is it?

**Buddy** It's not much.

*He gives her a box, smaller than a matchbox. She opens it. Inside, bits of crumbling grey rock, almost dust.*

**Jane** It's really lovely. That's really lovely, Buddy, thank you. A box of dirt.

**Buddy** Mmmhmm.

**Jane** Oh no.

**Buddy** Mmmhmm.

**Jane** Oh come on, it's not.

**Buddy** If it's not, throw it away.

**Jane** Look, I can't take this. If it is, I can't take it. Is it?

**Buddy** If you don't believe it is, then it may as well not be.

*She closes the box very carefully.*

**Jane** It's just a bit of earth, isn't it.

**Buddy** Would that make it any less valuable?

*He rises.*

**Buddy** Come on, I'll see you home.

*They leave the beach.*

**David** *moves away from* **Brenda**.

**Brenda** Where are you going?

**David** Walk along the beach.

**Brenda** It's hard to tell in this light if the tide's coming in. You could get cut off if the tide's coming in.

**David** What if it's going out?

**Brenda** Oh, then you'd walk all the up and around.

*And so* **David** *leaves.*

**Brenda** But what if it's not? What if it's not?

*Lights fade.*


Scene Four

*Sunrise.*

*Lights up in living room.* **Tom** *drinks coffee with* **Jane**, *who sits with her bag.* **Tom** *is dressed as a woman.*

**Tom** Brenda was the last to see him, and so you see how hard it would have been, to admit that and drag her back into the nightmare of police and gossip and some other man from some other paper.

**Jane** Do you think he drowned?

**Tom** There's more chance he beat the tide and just kept on walking.

**Jane** He hates walking. Where would he walk to?

**Tom** I think he realised he had some serious work to do. On himself.

**Jane** But he left me.

**Tom** Yes.

**Jane** A fine change of life. Leave the wife. Very original. What a shitheel. I mean seriously, isn't he? Stupid bastard.

**Tom** Well, he's not all bad.

**Jane** I know that, but he'll need more than heroic tales of hamster rescue when I see him again. Oh Christ. I might never see him.

**Tom** That's true.

**Jane** I'm a grown woman, it's absurd. I ought to be able to cope without one bloody man. Especially him. Why is it so hard?

**Tom** I've never understood why people get so painfully bound up with one person and remain so horribly disconnected from everyone else.

**Jane** A taste of heaven and a taste of hell. Why are you dressed as a woman?

**Tom** God, is that the time? I've got to get to the pub. They've got a stag lunch on.

**Jane** What are you, the cabaret?

**Tom** No, some poor half-naked woman is the cabaret. I am the raising of the consciousness! Bye bye.

**Jane** Bye.

**Tom** *leaves.*

*Lights up on the beach.* **David** *walks on, no jacket, no socks. A weary traveller.*

**Jane** *takes the box out of her pocket, and stirs the dust with her finger.*

**David** *takes his shoe off and pours from it a fine long trickle of sand.*

**Brenda** *comes on to feed the animals.* **Jane** *changes into walking boots.*

**Brenda** Oh. You're off then.

**Jane** Yes. Along the beach. David went north, didn't he?

**Brenda** Yes.

**Jane** Then I'll go south.

**Brenda** Don't want to catch him up then?

**Jane** Don't want to waste my life chasing him. Oh, by the way.

**Jane** *takes the half-deflated globe from her pocket. Blows it up.*

*At the same time* **David** *takes deep breaths of ocean air.*

**Jane** *hands the globe to* **Brenda**.

**Jane** I found this. For the kids?

**Brenda** Oh, ta. I wondered what had happened to that.

**Jane** *leaves.* **Brenda** *sits with globe. She walks the fingers on her right hand southwards, then the fingers on her left go north. They meet and intertwine, satisfied. Lights fade.*

# Hysteria

*or Fragments of an Analysis of an*
*Obsessional Neurosis*

# Setting

*1938*

*Sigmund Freud's study at 20, Maresfield Gardens, Hampstead, London. A large, high-ceilinged room plastered in pastel-blue. The room is furnished richly: dark oaks and mahogany.*

*US French windows lead to a narrow porch and beyond, a well-kept garden.*

*USR the door to a closet. SR a large desk. DSR a wood-burning stove.*

*Along the wall SL, an armless analysis couch covered with a rich Moroccan rug and half a dozen cushions. On the wall above, another beautiful rug. Just beyond the head of the couch, a comfortable tub chair.*

*DSL the door to the rest of the house.*

*There are bookshelves holding fine embossed volumes, and every available surface holds antiquities from ancient Greece, Rome, Egypt and the Orient. The vast majority of these are small human figures in pottery, wood and bronze.*

*The setting should be naturalistically rendered to contrast with the design challenge towards the end of Act Two.*

## Characters

| | |
|---|---|
| **Sigmund Freud** | *An energetic old man.* |
| **Jessica** | *A woman in her late twenties or early thirties.* |
| **Abraham Yahuda** | *A large man in his sixties. An even greater weight and status than Freud.* |
| **Salvador Dali** | *A small tall Spaniard with a strange moustache and a talent for painting.* |
| Figments | *Love, Death, Guilt, Fear, etc . . .* |

The style of the playing varies as Freud's last thoughts, recent memories and suppressed anxieties dictate the action.

*Hysteria* was first staged at the Royal Court Theatre, London, on 26 August 1993, with the following cast:

| | |
|---|---|
| **Sigmund Freud** | Henry Goodman |
| **Jessica** | Phoebe Nicholls |
| **Abraham Yahuda** | David de Keyser |
| **Salvador Dali** | Tim Potter |

*Directed by* Phyllida Lloyd
*Designed by* Mark Thompson
*Lighting Design by* Rick Fisher
*Sound Design by* Paul Arditti

# Act One

## Scene One

*Night. Rain beyond the windows.*
**Freud** *asleep in the tub chair. Wakes and looks at his watch. A long silence.*

**Freud** If you are waiting for me to break the silence you will be deeply disappointed. The silence is yours alone, and is far more eloquent than you imagine.

*He turns in his chair and looks towards the couch. Double-takes when he sees there is no one on it. Looks around the room. Opens the door, peers out, closes the door. Goes to his desk. Hesitantly presses the buzzer on an unfamiliar Bakelite intercom.*

**Freud** Anna?

**Anna** (*a voice pulled from sleep*) Yes, father?

**Freud** She's gone.

**Anna** Who, father?

**Freud** Where's she gone?

**Anna** Where's who gone?

**Freud** It's um . . .

*Looks at his watch.*

**Anna** What is it?

**Freud** Ten to.

**Anna** It's ten to five. It's the middle of the night.

**Freud** There was a girl.

**Anna** Have you slept yet?

**Freud** I had a patient.

**Anna**  Maybe you dreamed her.

**Freud**  I don't dream patients, I dream surgeons and publishers.

**Anna**  Go to bed, father.

**Freud**  The nights are valuable.

**Anna**  Yahuda will be here for lunch, and you've an appointment immediately after.

**Freud**  I'll sleep in the morning. What's this thing?

*In front of his face hangs an electric light pull; a four foot cord with a brass knob on the end.*

**Anna**  What thing?

**Freud**  This thing hanging here in front of me. This thing in my hand.

**Anna**  Um . . .

**Freud**  It's just dangling here. It's got a nob on the end.

**Anna**  Mmm hmm?

**Freud**  What is it?

**Anna**  I've . . . no idea.

**Freud**  What am I supposed to do with it?

**Anna**  Shall I call the nurse?

**Freud**  Shall I give it a pull?

**Anna**  No, just . . . leave it alone, father.

*He pulls it. The lights go out.*

**Freud**  Scheisse!

**Anna**  Father?

**Freud**  The lights have gone out.

**Anna**  Oh . . . that!

**Freud**  Damn thing.

**Anna**  It's a light pull. Ernst put it up this afternoon.

*A crash of falling objects.*

**Anna**  Father?

**Freud**  I hate the dark.

**Anna**  You should be asleep.

**Freud**  I know what's in it.

**Anna**  You need more, not less, as time passes.

**Freud**  The body maybe. The mind more than ever
craves ... (*He switches on the light.*) Illumination.

**Anna**  Shall I come down?

**Freud**  No, I'm fine.

**Anna**  Goodnight then.

**Freud**  Goodnight.

*He switches off the intercom. Some of the antique figures on his desk
have been knocked over; he rights them.*
*He picks up his pen to write. Nothing comes. He gets up and lies on
the couch.*

**Freud**  I have been preparing, somewhat unsuccessfully,
for my death which Yahuda would have me believe is
imminent. I am inclined to agree with his diagnosis, but
this morbid preparation is ... difficult. I have never liked
waiting for trains; standing on the platform looking back
down the track: never a glance, of course, in the direction
of one's destination. Like all the trains I ever caught, this
one is running late. And so I wait. I re-arrange the luggage
at my feet; I unfold and refold my newspaper, failing to
find anything of interest, even though the headlines roar.
And over and over I mentally rehearse the panic of
boarding, check my watch with the clock, grow anxious and
inexplicably ... impatient. I prepare and yet remain

unprepared, because when the train arrives there is never time to button the jacket or check the ticket or even say a meaningful goodbye. So until my inevitably fraught departure, all I can do is wait, and re-arrange the luggage.

*His eyes have closed.*

*A pause, then a figure appears through the rain and stops outside the French windows.* **Jessica** *is sopping wet and initially appears waif-like. She wears a thin mackintosh. Her hair hangs dripping to her shoulders.*
*She taps on the glass.* **Freud** *opens his eyes. She taps again. He rises, disorientated, and discovers the source of the noise. She smiles.*

**Freud**  Go away. Go away. This is a private house, not Madame Tussauds. I admit I found it flattering when I arrived, this English passion for standing and staring, but I'd rather be melted down thank you, than have any more thumb-nails surreptitiously pressed into my flesh, so please . . . go away! Oh very well, stay where you are, catch your death for all I care. What do you want?

*He goes to his intercom. She raps frantically. He doesn't press the buzzer. She speaks. We don't hear her through the glass.*

**Jessica**  I have to speak to you.

**Freud**  What?

**Jessica**  I have to speak to you.

**Freud**  I can't hear you. Go away.

*Very matter-of-fact, she takes out a cut-throat razor and holds it to her wrist.*

**Jessica**  I have to speak to you.

**Freud** *looks away. Thinks. Then goes to the French windows and unlocks them. He steps back. She enters.*

**Freud**  Stop there! Stop.

*She stops. Closes the razor. Offers it to him. He takes it and secures it in a drawer.*

**Jessica**   I wasn't sure you'd let me in.

**Freud**   You're sopping wet.

**Jessica**   It's raining.

**Freud**   That rug is from Persia.

**Jessica**   You told me to stop.

**Freud**   Get off the rug.

**Jessica**   Here?

**Freud**   There. Good. How did you get into the garden?

**Jessica**   I climbed. Where the elm rests on the wall.

**Freud**   I'll have a tree surgeon to it first thing in the morning.

**Jessica**   Grazed my knee; look.

**Freud**   What are you, some sort of insomniac student?

**Jessica**   No.

**Freud**   You want me to read something you wrote?

**Jessica**   No.

**Freud**   Are you inebriated, irresponsible, rich? Is this a dare?

**Jessica**   No.

**Freud**   Do you know who I am?

**Jessica**   Oh yes.

**Freud**   Then what do you want?

**Jessica**   I don't know. I haven't yet decided.

**Freud**   Who are you?

**Jessica**   Don't you recognise me?

**Freud**   It feels as though I should.

**Jessica**   Yes, you should.

**Freud**   We've met?

**Jessica**   No, never.

**Freud**   Please. It's late. Who are you?

**Jessica**   I am your anima, Professor Freud.

**Freud**   My what?

**Jessica**   It's a psychological term denoting the denied female element of the male psyche.

**Freud**   I know what it is.

**Jessica**   Denied but desired.

**Freud**   Damn nonsense, that's what it is. Did *he* send you?

**Jessica**   Who?

**Freud**   The Lunatic. Jung the crackpot, friend of the Gods?

**Jessica**   No.

**Freud**   He did, didn't he? This is his feeble idea of a practical joke.

**Jessica**   No one sent me.

**Freud**   Due to my advancing years I am quite prepared to come up against the odd figment of my own imagination, but I have no time for flesh and blood imposters. And I certainly refuse to confront aspects of my personality I did not even propose! Anima is tosh. Archetypes are a theatrical diversion!

**Jessica**   I've not read much Jung.

**Freud**   Not much is too much. How long have you been in the garden?

**Jessica**   All night. Watching the house. The lights going out. Then one last light, illuminating you.

**Freud**   Perhaps you should sit. Judging from your behaviour so far you are either dangerously impulsive or pathologically unhappy.

**Jessica**   That's true.

**Freud**   Which?

**Jessica**   Both, I think. I have inverted morbid tendencies, I know. And a great deal of free-floating anxiety desperate for someone to land on. I am mildly dysfunctional, yes.

**Freud**   You have recently been in analysis?

**Jessica**   No, I've recently been in the library.

**Freud**   If you are looking for a doctor, I'm afraid I have to disappoint you. My health deteriorates daily. I cannot take any more patients. Those I see now will soon be abandoned. I cannot add to my unfinished business.

**Jessica**   What if I were desperate?

**Freud**   There would be no point; I could never conclude. I will give you the name of a good man.

**Jessica**   No. It's you I must see.

**Freud**   Then you must be disappointed. I shall call someone to show you out.

**Jessica**   Don't do that.

**Freud**   It's very late. I'm an old man.

**Jessica**   What's wrong with your mouth?

**Freud**   With this half, nothing. The other half I left in Vienna.

**Jessica**   How careless of you.

**Freud**   It's in a jar of formaldehyde. The surgery was drastic, but advisable.

**Jessica**   I think I'd rather die than have a piece of me removed.

**Freud**   Cancer cells develop a passionate urge to replicate. They abandon any concern for the function of their familial organ and strike out to conquer foreign tissue. They undermine the natural state, absorb and conquer! They are the National Socialists of human meat; best left, I felt, in Austria. Now, you must go.

**Jessica**   It's still raining.

**Freud**   How could you possibly get any wetter? If you want to get dry, get home.

**Jessica**   I have no home.

**Freud**   I must insist. This is improper.

**Jessica**   I'll show you improper.

*She takes off her coat.*

**Freud**   What are you doing?

*She takes off her dress.*

**Freud**   Please, I am perfectly aware you wish to gain my attention but this is highly inappropriate. I shall call my daughter.

**Jessica**   And how will you explain me?

**Freud**   There is nothing to explain.

**Jessica**   Naked and screaming?

**Freud**   She will understand.

**Jessica**   But will the inhabitants of West Hampstead?

**Freud**   Now stop this. Your behaviour is totally unacceptable!

**Jessica**   My behaviour, Professor Freud, is as you first diagnosed. It is desperate, as am I!

*She goes into the garden, still undressing.*

**Freud**   Come back inside!

**Jessica** (*off*)   Do I start screaming or will you give me one hour of your precious time?

**Freud**   I will not be blackmailed. Come out of the rain!

**Jessica** (*off*)   No. I shall stand here until I'm too wet to think. Too cold to care.

*Thunder.* **Freud** *takes her coat and pursues her. Brings her back inside, wrapped.*

**Freud**   Sit.

*He moves a chair nearer the stove and ushers her into it.*

**Jessica**   Thank you. I'm sorry.

*She cries.*

**Freud**   I shall try to help. But could we please remember this is my study, not some boulevard farce.

**Jessica**   This isn't your study. Your study was in Vienna.

**Freud**   Who are you?

**Jessica**   Is it the same?

**Freud**   Almost. In the Bergasse it wasn't as simple to walk out into the garden.

**Jessica**   Why?

**Freud**   I was on the second floor. And there were many more books.

**Jessica**   More?

**Freud**   I had to choose between books and the survivors.

**Jessica**   Who?

**Freud**   The figures.

**Jessica**   They're beautiful.

**Freud**   And buried, unseen for centuries. It would have been criminal to inter them again. It felt bad enough cramming them into rail crates for transportation. Each of them is quite unique but when packed in side by side, they lose their individual identities. Wrapped in newsprint they become ... faceless.

**Jessica**    Are you in pain?

**Freud**    Yes. Are you?

**Jessica**    Oh yes.

**Freud**    I cannot take you on. I have no ... time.

**Jessica**    It won't take long. I know what's wrong with me.

**Freud**    Self-analysis is rarely successful.

**Jessica**    You did it.

**Freud**    I had the advantage of being me.

**Jessica**    And you were all you had to go on. I've read your books. All of them.

**Freud**    Have you really?

**Jessica**    Yes.

**Freud**    Understand much?

**Jessica**    Most.

**Freud**    Hmph.

**Jessica**    I didn't much enjoy *Jokes and Their Relationship to the Unconscious*. If you were going to analyse jokes you might have chosen a couple that were funny. I suspect you've no sense of humour.

**Freud**    Nonsense. Only last week I was taken to the theatre and I laughed three or four times.

**Jessica**    What at?

**Freud**    I believe it was called *Rookery Nook*.

**Jessica**    Doesn't prove you've a sense of humour; proves you've a complete lack of taste.

**Freud**    It had a seductive logic, and displayed all the splendid – ha! – anal obsessions of the English.

**Jessica**    Frankly some of your concepts are funnier than your jokes.

**Freud**    For instance?

**Jessica**    Penis envy, for instance. How in a thousand years of civilized thought anyone could imagine a penis an object of envy is beyond me. Those I have seen erect and bobbing seem positively mortified at their own enthusiasm. The only one I ever saw flaccid looked like something that had fallen out of its shell. Euugh. Why would anyone envy a squidgy single-minded probiscus that thinks it's God's special gift to those without.

**Freud**    You say you've done no analysis?

**Jessica**    None.

**Freud**    I think you should begin as soon as possible.

*She lies on the couch.*

**Freud**    But not with me.

**Jessica**    Don't pretend you're not curious, Professor. You're longing to know what brought me here. There's nothing you'd like better than to see me barefoot in the head.

**Freud**    You are mistaken.

**Jessica**    Please.

**Freud**    If I were to listen to anything you had to say, I would do so only because you are obviously disturbed, and only on the understanding that what we were doing was an assessment pending a referral.

**Jessica**    All right.

**Freud**    Very well.

*He sits at the head of the couch.*

**Jessica**   How do we start?

*Pause.*

**Jessica**   I can't see you.

*Pause. She twists around. He looks at her with a well-practiced neutral expression.*

**Jessica**   That's the point is it? That's part of it?

*She lies back. Pause.*

**Jessica**   And silence? Is that part of it too? It is, isn't it? How many minutes of silence must you have endured?

*Sunrise happens; a shaft of red light and a burst of birdsong.*

**Jessica**   I don't know how to begin. I was born in Vienna twenty-nine years ago. I am an only child. My mother was beautiful, my father was the owner of a small print works and a temple elder. We lived in a tall, narrow house. It had four floors but not many more rooms; a strange house, as if built by a child, an unsteady tower of wooden bricks. My father had a bad hip; he couldn't climb stairs. He had a room made up in what was the parlour. This was his room, at the bottom of the house. Anyway, I grew. I grew up, as you can see.

*He makes a note.*

You made a note, I heard you scribble.

*She twists around.*

What did you write, what did I say?

*She gets the same neutral expression.*

I see. Well anyway, here I am. Should I talk about now or then? Past or present? Both, I know, I'm sure, but which end should I begin?

*She rubs briefly at the top of her breast, as if removing a splash of wine. A hysterical manifestation.*

Why am I here? I'm here because I was sent. I wouldn't
have come of my own accord. I have been married two
years and my husband is concerned for me. I would find it
flattering if it were not ... He worries about about my
appetite, which is small, but does not concern me. I eat no
more than I desire. My husband also wishes I spent more
time outdoors; I prefer it inside. It is merely a preference,
not an illness. So that's why I'm here. It is desired that I
eat like a horse and live like one too, in a field if possible.
If you could turn me into a horse my husband would be
overjoyed.

*She rubs.*

What has he told you?

*She gags.*

**Freud**   Would you like some water?

**Jessica**   No thank you. Don't stand up. I don't like the
outdoors. I don't need three enormous meals a day.

**Freud**   How long have you felt this way?

**Jessica**   A year. Maybe longer. Yes. Nearly two. It's
always longer than I remember.

**Freud**   When did it start?

**Jessica**   It developed. Nothing sudden, nothing ...

*She rubs. Shakes her stiff fingers.*

One just becomes happier indoors. Less interested in the
taste of food. Really, I wouldn't be here at all if it wasn't
for my wretched husband.

**Freud**   What is wrong with your hand?

**Jessica**   Didn't he tell you? The fingers of my hand. My
hand has been examined by specialists, neither could
explain the problem with my fingers.

**Freud**   What is the problem?

**Jessica**  We thought arthritis, but we're assured otherwise. These three fingers have grown stiff, you see. They bend at the joints but will not move apart. The hand still functions. I can use it. But it looks so . . . reptilian. It is intensely frustrating.

**Freud**  And there is no physiological impairment?

**Jessica**  None, I'm assured.

*She gags, then rubs.*

I'm sorry. Don't stand up. Well? Can you help me?

**Freud**  No. I cannot.

**Jessica**  I'm sorry?

**Freud**  It is now certainly time for me to go to my bed.

**Jessica**  That was hardly a full consultation Professor; we're barely beyond the symptoms.

**Freud**  I am as aware of the symptoms as you. And I am aware of the aetiology of your hysterical paralysis, as well as the traumatic triggers of your anorexia and agoraphobia.

**Jessica**  So soon?

**Freud**  I know these things not because your compulsive behaviour is unconvincing or because I am capable of completing an analysis in less than ten minutes, but because I published the facts of this case thirty years ago, and you no doubt, judging by your excellent knowledge of them, read it only recently. Now I am very tired, both of your games and of this evening . . .

**Jessica**  Please, don't call anyone.

**Freud**  Either you leave, this instant, or I'll wake the house.

**Jessica**  It was a stupid thing to do. I'm sorry.

**Freud**  What do you take me for?

**Jessica**   It's a case history that interests me, that's all.

**Freud**   So you are a student.

**Jessica**   Yes. Yes, I am.

**Freud**   Then your methods of study are most unorthodox.

**Jessica**   May we discuss the case of Rebecca S.?

**Freud**   Certainly not. You disturb me, you attempt to deceive me . . .

**Jessica**   Did I?

**Freud**   What?

**Jessica**   Deceive you?

**Freud**   Not for very long.

**Jessica**   I did though, didn't I? The gagging and the . . .

*She rubs.*

Was that how she . . . ?

**Freud**   I was very explicit in my descriptions. You were very accurate in your impersonation.

**Jessica**   Spooky.

**Freud**   Now if you've had your fun . . .

**Jessica**   Listen. I know I'm a fool. But Rebecca means a lot to me. She's the basis of my thesis. Please.

**Freud**   You have forfeited any right to my time and attention. Now you may go into the garden and scream or dance with the spring fairies, I care not.

**Jessica**   What would Dr Jung say if he heard you mention fairies?

**Freud**   He'd probably take me down the path and attempt to introduce us. Now go home.

**Jessica**   Please . . .

**Freud**   Not one more word.

**Jessica**   I'll go then.

**Freud**   Good.

**Jessica**   Could I ask one thing of you?

**Freud**   One thing.

**Jessica**   Could you lend me a pair of wellingtons?

**Freud**   Wellingtons.

**Jessica**   My feet are freezing. No, it's too much to ask. I'm sorry; I'll be fine.

**Freud**   Wait there.

**Jessica**   No really, I couldn't.

**Freud**   It's a small price.

**Jessica**   A pair of socks would be heaven; those thick sort of woolly ones.

**Freud** *leaves.*

*Her manner changes. She attempts to open the filing cabinet, but finds it locked. Looks for and finds the key, hung staff-like on the arm of one of the figures.*

*The sound of a door off alerts her. Thinking quickly, she opens the French windows wide, then hides in the closet.*

**Freud** *returns, with boots and walking socks, to find her gone. Stands at the French windows for a while, until his confusion turns to philosophical acceptance. He closes the windows and leaves his study, switching off the light.*

**Jessica** *comes out of the closet. Turns on the angle-poise. Takes a journal out of her coat pocket, and carefully puts it on the desk. Then she opens the filing cabinet and looks under F. Takes out a maroon file of flimsy carbon copies of correspondence.*
*Settles down to work her way through the correspondence; a concentrated, obsessive search . . .*

*Lights fade.*

**Scene Two**

*Late afternoon.* **Jessica** *has gone, as have the wellingtons. The room is reasonably tidy.*

*Door opens and in marches* **Yahuda**, *an elderly Jewish doctor. He clutches a visiting bag and a bound document.*
**Freud** *follows.*

**Yahuda**   No, no, no. I'm not here to debate with you. No one in your family, no friend, colleague or critic has ever convinced you you were wrong about anything. I'm quite happy to be argued into my grave, but I'm not about to be argued into yours. I did you the courtesy of reading this . . . babble, now you will do me the courtesy of listening.

**Yahuda** *stops at a chessboard in play and takes a move he's already prepared.*

**Freud**   I had wondered at your silence during lunch.

**Yahuda**   Being polite has given me indigestion. We are both old men.

**Freud**   Time is short.

**Yahuda**   I shall allow your ill health to temper my anger, but not to lessen my resolve. I shall not leave this room until you have agreed not to publish this work.

**Freud**   My friend . . .

**Yahuda**   That remains to be seen.

**Freud**   I see.

**Yahuda**   The first paragraph made my blood run cold. 'If Moses was an Egyptian . . .'

**Freud**   If.

**Yahuda**   You do not mean the 'if', Freud. None of your ifs are questions; all your ifs are excuses for the outrageous statements they precede. Your proposal is that the man who gave us the word of God, the founder of the Jewish nation was an Egyptian aristocrat.

**Freud**   A simple reading of the facts . . .

**Yahuda**   You deny his origins . . .

**Freud**   Any intelligent analysis . . .

**Yahuda**   You undermine the core of the myth!

**Freud**   Myth, precisely.

**Yahuda**   The symbolic expression . . .

**Freud**   The reflection of an inner desire . . .

**Yahuda**   Of a basic truth . . .

**Freud**   A perversion of truth, an attempt to satisfy . . .

**Yahuda**   Moses was a Jew! Moses was chosen! If Moses was not a Jew, then we were not chosen! He was a Jew as I am a Jew. And you?

**Freud**   I have never denied, ever denied . . .

**Yahuda**   Well deny Moses and you deny us! At this time, of all times.

**Freud**   Yes.

**Yahuda**   When the little we have is being wrenched from us.

**Freud**   I know.

**Yahuda**   At this most terrible hour . . .

**Freud**   I take away our best man.

**Yahuda**   This is dreadful stuff. It is irreligious, unforgivably ill-timed, badly argued piffle.

**Freud**   But apart from that, what did you think?

**Yahuda**   There can be no discussion. You may not publish.

**Freud** *takes a move on the chessboard.*

**Freud**   Yahuda, you are a scholar. A believer I know, but a scholar all the same. And you do not believe that the Red Sea parted . . .

**Yahuda**   The this and that of the event . . .

**Freud**   Or that a babe floated down a river in a basket . . .

**Yahuda**   Are lost in the mist, the history. The mystery . . .

**Freud**   A babe in a basket would have drowned as sure as our nation on the ocean floor.

**Yahuda**   The myth, Freud.

**Freud**   You know these things for what they are.

**Yahuda**   The myth is what's important.

**Freud**   Have you been talking to the Lunatic?

**Freud** *discovers the filing cabinet key on his desk. This begins to preoccupy him.*

**Yahuda**   Remove the essence of the myth and you undermine the foundation of our faith. As indeed you seem intent on doing. Here. Right here. 'Religion is the neurosis of humanity'! You presume to find no evidence of God but in the heads of men. In the imaginings of desperate minds. And what is a mind, according to you people? Sparks in the brain.

**Freud**   And a little history.

**Yahuda**   Well, God is more than meat and electricity. Or the sufferings of a child, or the arrogance of a traitor Jew.

**Freud**   What alternative are you suggesting? That I censor my last thoughts? No. God is no more light in this darkness than a candle in a hurricane; eventually he will be snuffed out. But if one man's denial can explode him then that tiny conflagration would be a light far brighter than the guttering hopes he kindles in us. The death of God would light us not to hell or heaven, but to ourselves. Imagine. That we begin to believe in ourselves.

**Yahuda**   Damn yourself if you must.

**Freud**   I have to publish.

**Yahuda**   But remember one thing.

**Freud**   What?

**Yahuda**   You are not the only Jew who will die this year.

*The pain* **Freud** *has been suppressing overwhelms him. He fights and defeats it.*

**Yahuda**   Sigmund? Are you in pain?

**Freud**   Most uncalled for.

**Yahuda**   I shall examine you.

**Freud**   We both know what you'll find.

**Yahuda**   A man in your condition should be making peace with his God and his fellow man. Not denying one and outraging the other. Fetch a towel.

**Freud** *goes to the closet.*

**Freud**   I have spent my life standing up to unpleasant truths . . .

*He opens the closet. An arm comes out and gives him a towel.*

Thank you.

*He closes the door.*

. . . But it has never been my desire to offend . . .

*Stops. Realizes. Looks back.*

**Yahuda**   Know this, Freud. Unless you reconsider, you lose my friendship.

**Freud**   Good God.

**Yahuda**   Harsh, I know, but there it is.

**Freud**   Get out.

**Yahuda**   No need to be offensive.

**Freud**   No, not you.

**Yahuda**   Then who?

**Freud**   What?

**Yahuda**   You said: 'get out!'

**Freud**   Indeed. Get out . . . your things. Get your things out of your bag. And please, examine me.

**Yahuda** *takes an instrument from his bag, and peers into* **Freud**'s *mouth.*

**Yahuda**   Be certain of one thing; there is precious little I would not do to prevent you publishing. If you had the clap I'd hang the Hippocratic oath and seriously consider blackmail. But not you of course. Guiltless. Half a century of meddling in other people's passions, countless female patients lying there in front of you, and never a whisper of impropriety. No scantily-clad secrets in your closet, more's the pity. Oh, for a scandalous lever to prize you off your pedestal.

**Freud**   Ont ee ihiculoh.

**Yahuda**   What?

**Freud**   Nothing.

**Yahuda**   That certain things are hidden from us . . .

**Freud**   Ot?

**Yahuda**   Does not deny their existence.

**Freud**   Ot hings?

**Yahuda**   The minds of men, the face of God. You devote

yourself to one invisible thing yet refuse to contemplate the other.

*Finishes the examination.*

**Yahuda**   It's as you thought.

**Freud**   Inoperable?

**Yahuda**   It's very deep now. I'm sorry.

**Freud**   No, if I had a God to thank, I would.

**Freud** *grimaces.*

**Yahuda**   That's me prodding around. A pressure bandage?

**Freud**   Thank you.

**Yahuda** *removes from his bag a bicycle pump, a puncture repair outfit and an inner tube.*

**Freud**   What do you intend doing with that?

**Yahuda**   Mend my bike.

*Finds the bandage. Ties it tight around **Freud**'s jaw, with a bow on the top of his head.*

**Yahuda**   Of course, two centigrams of morphine . . .

**Freud**   No.

**Yahuda**   Just the one?

**Freud**   Absolutely not. I would rather think in pain than dream in oblivion.

**Yahuda**   Continue being a stubborn irreligious fool and oblivion's precisely where you're headed.

**Freud**   I cannot end with an act of disavowal.

**Yahuda**   Then end in silence.

**Yahuda** *moves to the closet.*

**Freud**   No!

**Yahuda**   What?

**Freud**   Don't go in there.

**Yahuda**   I need to wash my hands.

**Freud**   Please. Use the one across the hall. This we use now as a closet. So much correspondence, so many books . . .

**Yahuda**   Hmm.

**Yahuda** *heads for the door. Stops on his way to examine the chessboard. Almost takes a move, but stops himself.*

**Yahuda**   You think everyone but you is a complete fool.

*Exits.* **Freud** *rushes to the closet and flings open the door.*

**Freud**   You said you were going, I thought you were gone.

**Jessica** *appears wearing her raincoat and wellingtons.*

**Jessica**   Get rid of your visitor, Professor. We have work to do.

**Freud**   We have no such thing. I have other appointments.

**Jessica**   Cancel them.

**Freud**   I said I would arrange a referral.

*She goes back into the closet.*

**Freud**   Would you please come out of there! Very well, you give me no choice . . .

*He steps towards the closet.*
*The raincoat hits him full in the face.*

**Freud**   My God.

**Yahuda** *enters through the other door.* **Freud** *closes the closet door.*

**Yahuda**   I left my bike in the garden. I'll fix the puncture then I'll be off.

**Freud**    Good.

**Yahuda**    And you've another visitor; some Spanish idiot with a ridiculous moustache. Dilly, Dally?

**Freud**    Dali.

**Yahuda**    Doolally by the look of him.

**Freud**    The painter.

**Yahuda**    Really? If you want a physician's advice, you're not up to it. You should be resting, not entertaining foreigners.

**Freud**    A favour for a friend.

**Yahuda**    Whose is that?

**Freud**    Mine.

**Yahuda**    Is it raining?

**Freud**    Usually.

**Yahuda**    Looks all right to me.

**Freud**    The forecast was ominous.

**Yahuda**    Indoor storms imminent?

**Freud**    Yes. No. A possibility of flash flooding.

**Yahuda**    Damn. I'll bring my bike inside.

**Freud**    No.

**Yahuda**    I can't mend it in the rain.

**Freud**    It's not raining.

**Yahuda**    You said it was just about to.

**Freud**    No, I said there was the possibility of some weather. They weren't precise as to which sort.

**Yahuda**    Looks awfully small for you.

**Freud**   It shrank.

**Yahuda**   When the last flash flood came thundering through your study, I suppose?

**Freud**   Why don't you bring your bike through and mend it in the hall?

**Yahuda**   As you wish. Though upstairs might be best.

**Freud**   Upstairs?

**Yahuda**   To eliminate any danger of sudden drowning.

**Yahuda** *exits through the windows.* **Freud** *opens the closet to return the coat.*

**Freud**   Now please, I must insist that you come out of the closet.

**Jessica**   Whatever you say . . .

**Freud**   No. I mean, stay where you are, put your clothes back on and then . . .

*A wellington boot flies out, which he catches.*

Please. You must modify this behaviour immediately. This is a childish and ineffectual form of protest since I haven't a clue what you're protesting *about.*

**Jessica**'s *arm appears from the closet. Between her fingers, a letter of* **Freud**'s. *He moves until it's in front of his face, and starts to read it.*

I don't understand.

*She stuffs the letter right down into the boot.* **Yahuda** *re-enters pushing his bike and walking on one heel.*
**Freud** *closes the closet.*

**Yahuda**   You're overrun by snails; they're all over the path. I've trodden on half a dozen.

**Freud**   Please, the rug.

**Yahuda**   Could you take this for a second?

*He hands the bike to* **Freud**. *It is covered in snails and has a hot water bottle tied to the handlebars.*

**Yahuda**   Where's your boot-scraper?

**Freud**   We don't have a boot-scraper.

**Yahuda**   This is England for heaven's sake.

**Freud**   And every boot-scraper I encounter sends me flying out of someone's bloody conservatory!

**Yahuda**   I'll find a stick or something. There goes another one.

**Yahuda** *exits.*
**Freud** *puts the wellington on the floor and uses his free hand in an attempt to retrieve the carbon copy.*

*(off)*   What the devil? Freud! What's this?

**Freud** *rises, his arm inside the boot.*
**Yahuda** *re-enters with only one shoe on, hopping.*

**Freud**   What's what?

**Yahuda**   I don't know what you call the damn things. It was in the middle of your lawn. When I was a married man they were made of sterner stuff.

*Standing on one leg, he holds up* **Jessica**'s *slip. It falls in front of him.*

**Dali** *(off)*   No no no! Is all right; I see myself.

*A sharp knock on the door.*
*Enter* **Dali**. *A surprised pause, then sheer delight.*

**Dali**   So. Is true. What Dali merely dreams, you live! Maestro!

**Freud**   I can assure you there's a perfectly rational explanation.

**Dali**   He does not wish to hear it.

**Freud**   Who?

**Dali**  Dali.

**Freud**  Of course. Tell your Mr Dali I shall see him in just a few minutes.

**Dali**  But he is here.

**Freud**  I'm aware of that.

**Yahuda**  And there's more of it, underwear and all sorts.

**Freud**  It must have blown off the line. I'll be a few minutes.

**Dali**  No, but he is here.

**Yahuda**  There is no line.

**Freud**  I know he's here, I heard you the first time. Ask him to wait a few minutes.

**Yahuda**  Whose is it?

**Dali**  But wait he cannot. He is here.

**Freud**  Look dammit . . .

**Dali**  I am he.

**Freud**  Oh, I see.

**Yahuda**  I'll put it on the compost.

**Freud**  No! Give it to me.

**Yahuda**  It's not yours is it?

**Freud**  Yes. No. It's . . . my daughter's.

**Yahuda**  Anna's? At her age she should be dressing for warmth.

*He drapes the slip over **Freud**'s arm and exits on his heel.*

**Freud**  You are he.

**Dali**  And he is honoured.

*A crunch. **Yahuda** slips.*

**Yahuda**   Oh shit. There goes another one.

**Dali** *sits, pulls out a pad.*

**Dali**   You will not object?

**Freud**   What?

**Dali**   A first impression.

**Freud**   Ah.

**Dali** *sketches.*

It's not my bike. And my physician has piles, thus the . . .

*Hot water bottle.*

As for the snails . . .

**Dali**   Dali is passionate with snails.

**Freud**   For, you mean.

**Dali**   For, with, Dali's passions knows no bounds.

**Freud**   They just . . . took a liking to the bike I suppose.

**Dali**   You have a head like a snail.

**Freud**   Thank you very much.

**Yahuda** *re-enters with a clean shoe and more clothing.*

**Yahuda**   You want the rest?

**Freud**   Yahuda, this is um . . .

**Dali**   Dali.

**Yahuda**   We met in the hall. Has Anna lost a lot of weight in the last week?

**Dali**   You suffer from piles.

**Yahuda**   How extraordinarily acute of you.

**Dali**   Dali suffers also.

**Yahuda**   I know; I've seen your pictures.

**Dali**   You do not like the work of Dali?

**Yahuda**   You want a frank answer?

**Dali**   Always.

**Yahuda**   I find your work explicitly obscene, deliberately obtuse, tasteless, puerile and very unpleasant to look at.

**Dali**   What is not to like in this?

**Yahuda**   I think I'll leave you to it, Freud.

**Dali**   This is the man; the only man who can fully appreciate the genius of Dali's spontaneous method of irrational cognition and his critical interpretive association of delusional phenomena. Wait.

*Exits.*

**Yahuda**   You want some advice?

**Freud**   What?

**Yahuda**   Don't let him get on the couch.

**Dali** *enters with a finished canvas. 'Metamorphosis of Narcissus'.*

**Dali**   Is for you. Now you tell me. Look closely, and tell me . . . from what does Dali suffer?

**Freud**   Eyesight?

**Dali**   Is true. This man is genius.

**Yahuda**   Excuse me, I have an operation to perform.

**Freud**   Please, don't feel you have to . . .

**Yahuda**   No, no. I'm sure you two have much to discuss. Here.

*Offers* **Freud** *a bundle of underwear.*

**Freud**   Thank you.

**Yahuda**   I'm damned if I can imagine her in them. In fact I'm grateful I can't imagine her in them. I'll see you when he's gone.

*Exit* **Yahuda** *with his bike.* **Dali** *resumes his sketch.*

**Freud**   I'd really rather you didn't.

**Dali**   A thought, an idea from your head, it belongs to you. But your image belongs to Dali. Please.

**Freud**   I must insist. Put your pencil away.

**Dali**   You neither do not like the work of Dali?

**Freud**   Not if I am to be the subject. If I'd known this was your intention . . .

**Dali**   Please. Dali has no intentions, only intent.

*He puts his pad down.*

**Dali**   I have come to salute you . . .

**Freud**   Please don't bother.

**Dali**   . . . on behalf of all true disciples of the critical-paranoiac school of paint.

**Freud**   Who are they?

**Dali**   Dali. He is the only true disciples.

**Freud**   I see.

**Dali**   You are held in great esteem. We, by which I mean Dali and I, are engaged in a great struggle, to drag up the monstrous from the safety of our dreams and commit to the canvas. It is you have inspired this.

**Freud**   I am most flattered.

**Dali**   You say to dream, and there to search . . . is what I do. You say paranoia it transform reality to conform with the unconscious obsession, yes? So Dali gazes; is turned to stone, but, and an egg. Narcissus flowers from the egg. Desiring to be reborn he only gazes at himself and dreams of death. Life in this state is as unlikely as a flower from an egg. Expressed with masterly technique and ingenious illusion of course, and this is what Dali does, and only him. Would you like me to hang him?

**Freud**  Oh please, don't bother yourself.

**Dali**  Is no bother. Is an honour. I put it here.

**Freud**  That's a Picasso.

**Dali**  Picasso is Spanish. (*Removes painting.*) So is Dali.

**Freud**  You like Picasso?

**Dali**  Picasso is genius. (*Tosses painting.*) So is Dali.

**Freud**  I much admire 'Guernica'.

**Dali**  Picasso is communist.

**Freud**  Yes.

**Dali**  Neither is Dali.

**Freud**  You'll have to forgive me for being frank. I am in a certain amount of pain.

**Dali**  Divine.

**Freud**  Distracting. It's been a pleasure to meet you.

**Dali**  No. Dali cannot go. Not so soon. Let me describe to you the painting I have just completed. It is called . . . 'Dream Caused By The Flight Of a Bee Around a Pomegranate One Second Before Waking Up'. It depicts the splitting of a pomegranate and the emergence of a large gold fish. From the mouth of the fish leaps a tiger. From the mouth of the tiger leaps . . . another tiger. From the mouth of this tiger, a rifle with fixed bayonet about to pierce the white flesh of a naked girl, narrowly misses her armpit. Beyond all this a white elephant with impossible legs carries past a monument of ice.

*Pause.*

You have to see it for yourself, really.

**Freud**  Again, forgive my lack of courtesy . . .

**Dali**    Please, have none.

**Freud**    Very well. I have always thought the surrealist movement a conspiracy of complete fools. But as you had the audacity to elect me some sort of patron saint, I thought it only polite to meet you. I now find I lack the energy even to be polite.

**Dali**    Excellent! Dali has no concern for your health, no desire to be liked, and no manners. Creatures who live in the shell, Dali eats.
Until the moment he dies, he does as he please. And he refuses to leave.

**Freud**    I don't think I've ever met a more complete example of a Spaniard.

**Dali**    Do you mind if I examine your room?

**Freud**    Yes.

**Dali**    But I must.

**Dali** *looks around the room. Very nosey.*

**Freud**    I suppose the war has brought you to England?

**Dali**    In Spain until one week ago, Dali paint and is contemptuous of the Fascist machine rolling towards.

*He toys with the light pull, threatening some antiquities as if they were bar skittles.*

**Dali**    Then he think; no, this is all getting too historical for Dali. Immediately the desire to leave is enormous, and acted upon immediately.

**Freud**    Have you any idea when the desire to leave here might become at all substantial?

**Dali**    When Dali, being here with you, no longer feels real to Dali.

**Freud**    Shouldn't take too long then?

**Dali**    Please. Your life is almost over. Don't waste your precious time trying to analyse Dali; he is completely sane. In fact, the only one.

**Dali** *finds a snail on* **Freud**'s *desk.*

Hello, little snail.

*He unsticks it, prizes it from its shell with the point of his pencil, and eats it.*

It's not good. What sort of snail is this?

**Freud**    English garden.

*Swallows it.*

**Dali**    Is tasteless. Typical English.

**Freud** *finds another snail, which he deposits in a wastepaper bin with a clonk. This may happen several more times in the course of the play.* **Dali** *continues to look around, arrives at the closet and opens the door.* **Freud** *looks up.*

**Freud**    N ... er. ...

**Dali** *looks inside the closet and turns to stone himself. He closes the door, goes to* **Freud** *at the desk. Leans on the desk. Opens his mouth, closes it. Goes back to the closet. Opens it, goes inside, closes door behind him.*

**Dali** *(off)*    Buenos dias, mi amor. Eres hermosa y yo soy un genio!

**Jessica** *(off)*    How dare you.

*A muffled blow, a cry and a crash.* **Dali** *emerges holding his genitals. Unable to speak for some time.*

**Dali**    The girl in your closet.

**Freud**    Yes?

**Dali**    A hallucination, no.

**Freud**    No? I mean, girl? What girl?

**Dali**    In the closet.

**Freud**   There's a girl in my closet?

**Dali**   Naked girl.

**Freud**   Nonsense. She must be a figment of your unique imagination.

**Dali**   She kick me in the phallus.

**Freud**   An impressive hallucinatory sensation.

**Dali**   I have pain in the testicle.

**Freud**   Hysterical.

**Dali**   No, is not funny.

**Freud**   Obviously you are at the peak of your imaginative powers.

**Dali**   You think?

**Freud** *leads him to the door.*

**Freud**   Your fantasies have grown so undeniable, they push through the fabric of reality. It is imperative you return home and paint at once.

**Dali**   A naked girl in the closet of Freud with the hooves of a stallion; is good.

**Freud**   Visionary.

**Dali**   I shall dedicate to you.

**Freud**   Thank you. Goodbye.

**Dali**   The pain is transformed; is divine.

**Freud**   So good to have met you.

**Dali**   The honour, it is Dali's. I owe you my life.

**Freud**   An unintentional gift, I assure you.

**Dali**   Goodbye!

*He leaves.*

**Freud** *grabs the clothing and has his hand on the closet door handle when* **Dali** *re-enters.*

**Dali**    No, no, no, no, no! I cannot leave.

**Freud** *hides the clothing behind his back.*

**Freud**    Please, be firm in your retholution. Resolution.

**Dali**    Dali is firm in his trousers. His pain has transformed, his member tumescent. Dali is obsessed. The vision in the closet must be his. He must look again.

**Freud**    No.

*Enter* **Yahuda. Freud** *spins.*

**Yahuda**    Anna's? I think not. Give them to me.

**Freud**    The what?

**Yahuda**    The flimsies.

**Freud**    I don't have them.

*But* **Dali** *can see them, and pounces.*

**Dali**    Ahah! The garments of the Goddess.

*He takes the bundle and buries his face.*

**Yahuda**    Has he met your daughter?

**Dali**    She is a feast; you smell.

**Yahuda** *takes the bundle.*

**Yahuda**    I'll do no such thing. Freud, there's about enough silk here to barely cover Anna's left shin. I intend to confront her with these.

**Freud**    Ah.

*He heads for the door.*

**Yahuda**    And you'd better hope for a positive identification.

**Freud**    No, Yahuda ... !

**Dali**   She fill my senses!

*He throws off his jacket, grabs his pad, and opens the closet.*

**Freud**   No!!

**Freud** *rushes for the closet.* **Yahuda** *escapes.*

*Closet door closes behind* **Dali** *before* **Freud** *can get there. He rushes to the other door, but it closes behind* **Yahuda**.

**Dali** *(off)*   Ahh ... mi amor, mi amor!

*Vague Spanish rumblings.* **Freud** *approaches the door, curious. Puts his ear to it.*

**Jessica** *(off)*   See this?

**Dali** *(off)*   Si.

*The door flies open, hitting* **Freud** *on the jaw.* **Dali** *hurtles out, trips, and lands spectacularly, out for the count.*

**Jessica** *(off)*   I am a defenceless woman and refuse to be intimidated by amorous Spaniards!

**Freud**   His arousal is entirely your responsibility.

**Jessica**   A woman has the right to sit naked in a cupboard without being propositioned.

**Freud**   I would defend your right, but not your choice of cupboard. Should this man sadly regain consciousness, I can give you no guarantee of his behaviour unless you get dressed.

**Jessica**   Very well; give me my clothes.

**Freud**   Ah.

**Jessica**   What does that mean? Ah?

**Freud**   I have temporarily mislaid them.

**Jessica**   Then you'll have to take me as I come.

**Freud**   No! Wait. Here.

*Throws her* **Dali***'s jacket.*

**Jessica**   Thank you.

**Freud**   All right?

**Jessica**   Well, I don't think I'll get into the royal enclosure.

**Freud**   Please, stay hidden.

**Jessica**   If you swear to give me a hearing.

**Freud**   All right, I swear.

**Jessica**   When?

**Freud**   When Yahuda's gone. I'll give two knocks.

*He closes the door. It opens again.*

**Jessica**   It's bloody cold in here; I want more clothes.

**Freud**   All right! All right! I'll get you some. Just wait quietly.

**Freud** *closes the door on her again. Lifts* **Dali***'s head, looks in his eyes. Drops his head and starts to remove his trousers.*

*Enter* **Yahuda***.*

**Yahuda**   She's never seen them in her life.

*He sees* **Freud** *and* **Dali***. Pause.*

**Yahuda**   You and I have to have a serious chat.

**Freud**   I was just . . . removing his trousers.

**Yahuda**   So I see. He appears to be unconscious.

**Freud**   Exactly. He began hyperventilating and fainted. I'm loosening his clothing.

**Yahuda**   He breathes through his backside as well, does he?

**Freud**   He was complaining of abdominal pains.

**Yahuda**   Really?

**Yahuda**'s *professionalism takes over. He examines* **Dali**.

**Freud**   Most definitely. Indigestion maybe, but perhaps something very serious. Hopefully a ruptured appendix.

**Yahuda**   Hopefully?

**Freud**   Well I mean, something worth your rushing him to hospital for, but of course hopefully not, touch wood.

*Raps twice on the nearest bit of wood, which happens to be the closet door.* **Jessica** *comes out of the closet.* **Freud** *steers her back in and closes the door, stubbing her elbow.*

**Jessica**   Ow.

**Freud**   Ow. That was the sound he made, just before he collapsed.

**Yahuda** *rises.*

**Dali**   Owwww.

**Yahuda**   This man has suffered a blow to the head.

**Freud**   Yes. He was going into the garden and hit his head on the door frame.

**Yahuda**   As he fainted?

**Freud**   Yes.

**Yahuda**   Which?

**Freud**   Both.

**Yahuda**   That's not possible.

**Freud**   Yes it is. He was standing on the filing cabinet, fainted, and hit his head on the way down.

**Yahuda**   What was he doing on the filing cabinet?

**Freud**   I don't know. I wasn't here. I was already in the garden.

**Yahuda**  Doing what?

**Freud**  Chasing a swan.

**Yahuda**  Where did that come from?

**Freud**  I haven't the faintest idea. But it could have been the swan that entered the room very aggressively and forced Dali to retreat to the filing cabinet where he fainted in terror.

**Yahuda**  This is utter nonsense.

**Freud**  The answer is a sponge cake.

**Yahuda**  What?

**Freud**  Nothing.

**Yahuda**  Freud, you've finally lost your marbles. Sixty years of clinical smut has taken its toll. Cross-dressing, violent tendencies and attempted sodomy . . . I'll keep it quiet of course, but I don't think you'll be publishing much else.

**Freud**  That is slanderous! What proof have you?

**Dali**  Owww.

**Yahuda**  I'll get my bag. When he regains consciousness I shall find out exactly what's been going on here.

**Yahuda** *exits.*

**Freud** *close to panic. Knocks on the closet. Lifts* **Dali** *by the ankles.*

*The closet door remains closed. He drops* **Dali** *and knocks again. Lifts* **Dali** *by the ankles. The door remains closed.*

**Freud** *goes to the door.*

**Freud**  Open the damn door.

*The door opens. He gets* **Dali** *by the ankles and slides him towards the closet.*

**Freud**   I gave the signal.

**Jessica**   You hurt my elbow.

**Freud**   Two knocks is the signal.

**Jessica**   That's what you did, and I came out and look at my elbow.

**Freud**   Not one knock, not three knocks; two knocks.

**Jessica**   I'm not having him in here.

**Freud**   He's been rendered harmless. Just a few minutes, please.

**Jessica**   Added to those you already owe me.

*Closes door as* **Yahuda** *enters. Pause.*

**Yahuda**   Where is he?

**Freud**   He left.

**Yahuda**   He what?

**Freud**   Through the garden, went over the wall. What a morning. You were right, I should be resting.

**Yahuda**   He was only half conscious.

**Freud**   Self-induced trance; he uses it to paint.

**Yahuda**   Rubbish.

**Freud**   Exactly. How's your bike?

**Yahuda**   What about the underwear?

**Freud**   What?

**Yahuda**   This stuff.

*Pulls it from his pocket.*

**Freud**   Ah.

**Yahuda**   Well?

**Freud**   What did I say last time?

**Yahuda**  You said it was your daughter's.

**Freud**  Utter nonsense. She's far too . . .

**Yahuda**  I completely concur.

**Freud**  But she's hoping to lose weight. These are a sort of incentive to diet.

**Yahuda**  What sort of a fool do you take me for?

**Freud**  Yahuda . . . The truth of the matter is . . . Um . . . The Spanish lunatic came early this morning; we had given him permission to paint in the garden. He brought with him a young lady, a professional model . . .

**Yahuda**  It's common knowledge Dali only ever paints his wife.

**Freud**  His wife. She was his wife. The model was. His wife the model. He set up his easel, she unfortunately disrobed. If we had known, it goes without saying. . . . They were discovered shortly before you arrived. To save you any embarrassment they were hurried indoors and Dali made a pretence of arriving after you.

**Yahuda**  She's Russian isn't she?

**Freud**  Wh . . . er?

**Yahuda**  Dali's wife.

**Freud**  She's er . . . is she? Is. Russian, yes.

**Yahuda**  Where is she now?

**Freud**  Oh, she . . . she left. Much earlier.

**Yahuda**  What was she wearing?

**Freud**  Um . . . I give up. What was she wearing?

**Yahuda**  Well not these, for a start.

**Freud**  Well no, but I lent her a jacket and . . . my wellingtons.

**Yahuda** *eyes the wellington.*

**Freud** She only took one.

**Yahuda** I see. And then presumably she hopped half-naked all the way down the Finchley Road?

**Freud** No, she hopped across the lawn to the laburnum bush beneath which she had previously concealed her clothes. Then she left.

**Yahuda** No one passed me.

**Freud** Ah, no; they climbed over the wall.

**Yahuda** What on earth for?

**Freud** They um, they're in training. They intend to climb a mountain together in the spring. A small Himalayan one. They're very adventurous and very in love.

**Yahuda** Oh well, that explains everything.

**Freud** Does it?

**Yahuda** I'm sure the Himalayas are knee-deep in fornicating Spaniards. Not to mention naked Russians looking for their wellington boots.

**Freud** Well, apparently this is so.

*Pause.*

**Yahuda** All right, I believe you.

**Freud** You do?

**Yahuda** I'd believe anything of the Godless avant-garde.

**Freud** *collapses with relief.*

**Yahuda** There's only one more thing you need to explain.

**Freud** Yes?

**Yahuda** *wanders to the closet. Raps it once with his knuckles. His hand waves through the air as if to rap again,* **Freud** *stiffens, but* *the hand becomes an accusing finger.*

**Yahuda**    What's in the closet?

**Freud**    Absolutely nothing.

**Yahuda**    Don't give me that; you've been buzzing around it like a blowfly.

**Freud** *joins him at the closet.*

**Freud**    Papers, papers, a life's work . . .

**Yahuda**    Open it up.

**Freud**    I've mislaid the key.

**Yahuda**    Open this door.

*He raps twice.* **Freud** *instantly adds a third rap. Grins inanely.*

**Yahuda** *frowns, suspicious. Raps twice again.* **Freud** *adds a third rap.*

**Yahuda** *raps once.* **Freud** *raps twice.*

**Yahuda** *dummies a rap.* **Freud** *raps twice, then hurriedly adds one.*

**Yahuda**    What in God's name is wrong with you?

**Freud** *is desperately trying to remember the count.*

**Yahuda** *raps again, once, and strides away.* **Freud** *in complete confusion adds another one, and also walks away. Then stops dead.*

**Freud**    Scheisse.

*The closet opens.* **Jessica**, *dressed in* **Dali**'s *clothes, walks out. Sees* **Yahuda**'s *back. As he turns, so does she, and attempts to return to the closet.*

**Yahuda**    Ahah! Stop where you are!

*She stops.*

Over the wall is he, Freud?

**Yahuda** *closes the closet to cut off her escape. She keeps her back to* *him.*

All right, you bohemian buffoon; what have you got to say for yourself?

*She shrugs.*

Don't give me any of your continental gestures. Just please inform me what sort of a relationship you have with this man.

*Another shrug.*

Turn around dammit and face me like a man.

**Jessica** *fiddles with her hair.*

**Yahuda**   I swear he's got shorter.

*She turns round. She's attempted to fashion herself a moustache. A pause.*

All right, Freud; over to you. Let's hear it.

**Freud**   Um . . .

**Jessica**   Dr Yahuda, the truth is . . .

**Freud**   You wish to speak to me!

**Jessica**   That's true.

**Freud**   So in order for our conversation to happen, you did not leave with your husband.

**Jessica**   Who?

**Freud**   Dali; your husband. Because you wished to speak to me.

**Jessica**   That's right. I didn't go with my husband Dali, Dali my husband because . . . (*Dreadful Spanish accent.*) . . . I thtayed behind to thpeak to Profethor Freud which ith why I wath thitting in the clothet.

**Freud**   Besides; you'd had a row.

**Jessica**   Ith correct.

**Freud**   And you hit him on the head.

**Jessica**   Thith ith true.

**Yahuda**   With a swan, presumably?

**Jessica**   Que?

**Yahuda**   May I ask you a personal question?

**Jessica**   Thertainly.

**Yahuda**   What country do you come from?

**Jessica**   Thpain, of courth.

**Freud** *behind* **Yahuda** *now, gestures frantically.*

**Jessica**   Not thpain? No, I hate thpain. Spain. Spain? Plagh!

**Yahuda**   So?

**Jessica**   Sssso . . . I come from . . .

**Freud** *tries to look like Lenin.*

**Jessica**   A very important city um . . . near Mount Rushmore. No, no. Only joking.

**Freud** *holds up an umbrella and with his curved arm, tries to make a hammer and sickle.*

**Jessica**   It rains a lot. Where I come from. England, it's . . . no.

*He stands in a Russian sort of way.*

**Jessica**   The people where I come from are very rugged because it rains so much.

*He slow marches.*

**Jessica**   In fact many of them are dead.

*He tries the same thing again, but more exaggerated.*

**Jessica**   Turkey? No. I'm just having you on. If you seriously want to know, um . . .

**Freud** *stabs at his head with a finger, impersonating Trotsky's death.*

**Jessica**   Where I come from . . . They're all mad. The entire country is completely barmy. France! It's France! I'm French! No I'm not, what a stupid thing to say.

*She's losing her patience with* **Freud**, *he's losing his with her. He stands with his finger on his head.*

**Jessica**   Mars. I come from Mars.

*He does a Russian dance.*

**Jessica**   Or Russia, I don't give a t . . . Russia! Russia? I come from Russia. That's where I come from. Russia.

**Yahuda**   Really?

**Jessica**   Oh yes. It's very warm for October isn't it? Precious little snow.

**Yahuda**   You don't sound Russian.

**Jessica**   Oh . . . *Vy mozhete skazat' mnye chuke proiti k zimnemu dvortcu? Dva kilograma svekly i butylku vodki. Da zdravstvuyet velikii Sovetskii Soyuz!* (Can you tell me the way to the Winter Palace? I would like half a pound of beetroot and a bottle of vodka, please. Long live the glorious USSR!)

**Freud**   Oh, bravo.

**Yahuda**   All right, I give up.

**Freud**   That was brilliant.

**Yahuda**   But you came close Freud, so be warned; I may be willing to suspend my disbelief this far, but not one step further.

**Dali** *comes out of the closet in his underwear.*

**Dali**   Excuse me please. Dali does not remove his clothings.

**Freud**   I can explain this.

**Dali**   Pretty girls remove their clothings for Dali, not versa vica!

**Freud**   In fact I can, I can explain this.

**Jessica**   I've had enough of this pathetic farce.

*She takes her clothes and goes back into the closet.*

**Yahuda**   Freud, will you tell me why on earth you are consorting with these lunatics?

**Freud**   Patients, Yahuda.

**Yahuda**   I've been patient long enough!

**Freud**   No, these are my patients.

**Yahuda**   Patients?

**Freud**   My last patients. A couple of mild cases to occupy my mind until . . .

**Yahuda**   I see. Now it all falls into place. You always were one for a challenge, weren't you?

**Freud**   You are a generous and understanding man.

**Yahuda**   Not at all.

**Dali**   You will pose for Dali, yes?

**Jessica** (*off*)   No.

**Dali**   Your armpit, it is divine. I must make unto it the graven image!

**Yahuda**   I'd better leave you to it then. Good afternoon.

**Freud**   Good afternoon.

**Yahuda**   I'll be back of course.

**Freud**   Mmm?

**Yahuda**   You know what for.

**Freud** *discerns something sinister in these parting words as* **Yahuda** *exits.*

**Jessica** *emerges, buttoning her dress.*

**Dali**  But your armpit; where is it?

**Jessica**  Under my arm. Professor Freud, I wish to continue the analysis.

**Freud**  Whose?

**Jessica**  The one we began.

**Freud**  What is the point? The details of the case are fully documented.

**Jessica**  Not only by you.

*She produces a small book.*

**Jessica**  This journal belonged to the patient you called Rebecca S. Her real name was Miriam Stein. This is the journal she kept of her work with you.

**Freud**  So?

**Jessica**  I'd like us to read it. I've simplified what she remembered of the sessions, and selected the most apposite passages. Please; read with me.

**Freud**  I have neither the time nor the inclination.

**Dali**  Please.

**Jessica**  What?

**Dali** *waves some money at her.*

**Dali**  To consider my request a professional proposition.

**Jessica**  No.

**Dali**  Name your price.

**Jessica**  I'm not for sale.

**Dali**  The armpit only. My Venus.

*He kisses her hand . . .*

**Jessica**  Professor?

**Freud**   It would be a pointless exercise.

*. . . and lifts her arm for a peek.*

**Jessica**   Get off!

**Dali**   On my knees.

**Freud**   I will have nothing to do with it.

**Dali**   Dali will do anything you ask.

**Jessica**   Can you read English?

**Dali**   Dali is perfect English. Not have got you ears?

**Jessica**   Very well. Read the passages underlined.

**Dali**   Que?

**Freud**   Look, I really must insist . . .

**Dali**   What for is this?

**Jessica**   We are going to reconstruct one of the Professor's case histories. You sit here. When we are finished you may have fifteen minutes to do what you will with my armpit.

**Dali**   Is a deal. I am to be the fraud of the great Freud, yes?

**Dali** *sits in the tub seat.*

**Freud**   No. I will not tolerate this.

**Dali**   Ah.

**Jessica**   What anxieties are prompting your objections, Professor? Read the passages marked with an F.

**Dali**   But if the Professor object to this worm presuming to embody him then this Dali cannot possibly . . .

**Jessica** *puts her hand behind her head.*

**Dali**   . . . refuse you my darling, and to hell with this man and his beard also.

**Freud**   Very well, if you insist. Get it over with.

**Jessica**   From the top of the page.

**Dali**   So. 'As you speak to me you will notice ideas will occur that you feel are not important, are nonsensical, not necessary to mention. But these disconnected things are the things you *must* mention.' Dali knows this; he has read this from the book. 'You must leave nothing unsaid, especially that which is unpleasant to say.' Maestro.

**Jessica**   Concentrate.

**Dali**   Of course.

**Jessica**   It's a warm day. I had difficulty getting here. The cab driver was reluctant to raise the canopy, and I cannot travel in an open cab.

*She rubs her breast.*

I don't like leaving the house. Walking across a field or a town square is a nightmare. I want to stick to the hedge or the edge of the wall, but even then there's this constant possibility . . . A wicker basket. Just came into my head. Is that the sort of thing?

**Dali** *is rubbing his nipple exotically.*

**Jessica**   What are you doing?

**Dali**   Is what it says here. I was gently rubbing my breast.

**Jessica**   Not your breast, my breast.

**Dali**   You rub the breast of the patient? Is not in the published works you did this.

*He reaches out, she slaps his hand.*

**Jessica**   She was rubbing her own breast.

**Dali**   Que?

**Jessica**   'I' is me.

**Dali**   Oh, *Si. Si.* Apologize. 'Continue'.

**Jessica**    When I was young we had a wicker basket; I used to play ships in it. It was a picnic basket. I don't know why I've thought of this, but . . . my mother reading to us, the story of Chicken Little. A piece of the sky falls on his head. Bits of the sky falling. I hate the sky, the way the clouds scud. Looking through my Grandmother's window. There's a birdcage next to me with a canary. It's got some sort of disease; its beak is being eaten away.

*Gags.*

Something I've just remembered, God it was horrible, and I'd forgotten all about it. I'm lying in my Grandmother's garden. I'm an adult, I'm nineteen and she's told me to wait for something spectacular. I remember this now. She said if I lay still I'd get a spectacular surprise. And I'm full of anticipation, waiting for her to bring out a cake or something and suddenly . . .

*She rubs.*

The air is full of birds. Starlings. Not just a few dozen but thousands. A black cloud of starlings. A tattered sky and those horrible birds just . . .

*She gags.*

I run inside. I'm really angry with her. And the starlings roost in trees all round the house and I sit curled up in a cold dark study in a leather chair and listen to the noise and I am terrified. Some of them swoop to the windowsill. My heart races. I'm scared of the starlings. I'm frightened of the birds.

**Dali** *applauds.*

**Jessica**    Don't do that.

**Dali**    It says this. There was applause.

*She takes the journal.*

**Jessica**    There was a pause.

**Dali**   I see, *si. Si.*

*Pause.*

**Dali**   In this pause you think maybe I light a cigar?

**Jessica**   No.

**Dali**   No, *si.*

**Jessica**   I don't know why but I'm thinking now of a flame, a small, a candle flame . . . and it's burning *upside down.* I don't understand that. A heavy sky. Leaden. I'm afraid of the sky. No I'm not. It's not the sky, is it? It's that a bird might fly, might pass overhead. Not all those starlings, something far worse; one bird in a blue sky. That's what frightens me. The *possibility* of a bird.

*She rubs.*

**Freud**   Are you finished?

**Jessica**   No. Later in that same first session, they discuss her eating disorder and she free associates around food and meals. I haven't learnt this bit. Give it to me.

*She reads.*

'Knife fork and spoon should be lined up just so. A knife should never be put into the mouth . . . all these rules my father had. Preparing for a picnic . . . the basket!' And eventually . . . here it is.

**Freud**   Look . . .

**Dali**   Please . . . shhh.

**Jessica**   'I am about seven years old. I am at the table. My father is giving a dinner party and I have begged to attend. I am on my absolutely best behaviour. The candles are lit and the mahogany shines. I ask my mother to pass the salt, even though my father disapproves of my using condiments. I tip the salt cellar, but nothing comes out. The salt is damp. I shake the salt cellar, only once, and the silver top flies off. Salt pours in a thick quick flow all over

my plate, all over my food, and flicks down the table as I
try to stop the flow. The guests turn as one to look at me.
Some laugh. I feel the most unbearable humiliation. My
ears burn. My mother brushes some of the salt into her
hand with a napkin, but the food is ruined. So I picked up
my knife and fork and I eat it. I pretend it does not taste
digusting. I eat until my mouth is dry, my gums are
stinging. Tears of shame and embarrassment spill down my
cheek. I run upstairs and vomit. Put myself to bed, the bed
is cold. I listen miserably to the guests leaving and pray my
father will be angry w . . . will *not* be angry with me.'
There was a silence, then you announced that the session
must come to a close. Then asked, as if in passing, how
often she had intercourse with her husband. She refused to
answer. She was pressured to do so.

**Freud**    Where is this leading? What is your point?

**Jessica**    I need to take this step by step. We shall leap to
another session; the sixth.

**Freud**    No. I refuse to participate any further.

**Jessica**    We're almost there.

**Freud**    Please. Leave.

*She opens a desk drawer and pulls out her razor.*

**Jessica**    I have to finish this. Help me finish it.

**Dali**    Please. I say something?

**Jessica**    Yes?

**Dali**    Goodbye.

**Jessica**    Stay where you are.

**Dali**    Just here?

**Jessica**    Just there.

**Dali**    Is good. Is very nice just here. No need to move at
all, never.

**Freud**  Put that down.

**Jessica**  Let me do what I have to do and then I swear, I'll disappear.

**Freud**  Very well, but give me the razor.

**Jessica**  No.

**Dali**  Is good to give it to him. Is better to keep it though. Wow, it's really nice just here, isn't it?

**Jessica**  Sit down. By this time her anorexia has been suspended. She's eating again, quite well. The gagging has greatly reduced; she has successfully related the gagging to the taste of salt, real or imagined, and thus to the trauma of the dinner party. From there.

**Dali**  'I wish you to concentrate on your fear of birds. What thoughts come to you?'

**Jessica**  The smell of leather. Mahogany. A candle flame. Of course, at the dinner party the candle flames were reflected in the polished wood. They were upside down.

**Dali**  'What of the birds?'

**Jessica**  Oh, birds, eggs, boiled eggs ... the picnic basket. I'm sick to death of that picnic bask...

**Dali**  A pause.

**Jessica**  I'm eating a boiled egg at a picnic. My whole family is there. My father has refused to undo his collar. It is very hot. He offers me salt in which to dip my egg. I of course decline. I'm in my late teens by now, I think of myself as very demure. I am dressed in white. And there are friends of the family there. This is more than a ... It was my father's birthday! I feel good towards him. I feel he likes me now. He gives me the odd stiff smile. I wish we were alone; I'm sure we could talk together now. I wish we were alone. A long way off a child is crying. A bird flies overhead. My father calls my name. Miriam. No! I look up and smile and *no*!

*She cries out in disgust. Rubs violently. Gags.*

It's all over me; my dress, my breast.

**Dali**    What is this?

**Jessica**    A bird, a filthy bird. A streak of white, a sudden flash of green, it's warm and wet and it's on my breast. An unspeakable mess; it's bird excrement.

**Dali**    'Relax.'

*The fit continues.*

'You are here, you are safe. He embraces her.'

*The fit continues.*

Is your line.

**Freud**    He embraces her!

**Dali**    Oh, *si*. Sorry. Is allowed?

**Freud**    Yes, is allowed.

**Dali** *embraces her. She calms down.*

**Jessica**    I wipe at the stuff with my fingers. It makes it worse. It's all over my fingers and my beautiful new ... breast. My father, thankfully, looks away embarrassed. He pretends he saw nothing. I try to clean up with a napkin but my dress is stained and however much I try to clean them, all afternoon my fingers feel ... sticky. Stuck together. All the way home, I hide my hand. And my father, all the way home, never once looks at me.

*Pause.*

Is that how it was? Her fit?

**Dali**    Was magnificent.

**Jessica**    Is that how it was?

**Freud**    Similar.

**Jessica**    And did you embrace her?

**Freud**   Yes.

**Jessica**   She says . . . (*Reads.*) 'I clung to him to prevent myself falling through the door that had opened up beneath me and through which I had seen that summer's day so clearly. And the door righted itself and I knew it was now my choice to step through and remember whatever I wished. I am so deeply and eternally grateful to this man.'

**Freud**   Transference is common to all successful analyses.

**Jessica**   They all fall in love?

**Freud**   Without exception.

**Dali**   Wow.

**Freud**   And the gift that must be returned is an acceptance of that love, with no love returned, no demands made, no respect diminished.

**Jessica**   You never loved in return?

**Freud**   Of course not.

**Jessica**   She felt euphoric at the revelations tumbling from her past. And the symptoms began to disappear. She recognized the wiping gesture for what it was, and laughed when she caught herself doing it. Life opened up she said, like a painted fan. What continued to disturb her were your questions about her intimate affairs. She had admitted her distaste for copulation and acknowledged her husband's frustration, but still every week you pushed, you probed, you insisted that she spoke of these things.

**Freud**   This is indelicate. I've had enough.

**Jessica**   We've reached the crucial session.

**Freud**   You will leave my house, please.

**Jessica**   What have you to hide?

**Freud**   Don't be impertinent. Whatever confidences you are about to reveal from this poor woman's private reminiscences, and whatever conclusions you may have reached, I can assure you that no impropriety took place between us. And no such impropriety has ever taken place between myself and any patient.

**Jessica**    I'm not accusing you.

**Freud**    But you were about to.

**Jessica**    It's obviously something you feel very defensive about . . .

**Freud**    How dare you!

**Jessica**    But I have no intention of making any such accusations.

**Freud**    Then what is this about?

**Jessica**    One more visit. The seventh. She returns. Things are not good. The gagging has returned and she finds it impossible to keep any food down. Her fingers are useless, and her wiping tic incessant and exaggerated. She's distraught that in spite of all she's learned, she's iller than ever.

**Freud**    When she arrived. Not when she left.

**Jessica**    She was very angry with you, very angry, and you sensed this. Didn't you?

**Freud**    Of course.

**Jessica**    And you encouraged her to express her anger, didn't you?

**Freud**    Of course.

**Jessica**    And did she? Did she? *Did she*?!

*She hits him.*

**Dali**    No.

**Freud**    It's all right. Yes she did.

**Jessica**    I'm almost there. Almost there now.

*The hysterical symptoms take hold of her, more exaggerated and more frequent. Other physical tics manifest themselves. She returns to the couch in an increasingly distressed state.*

**Dali**   Is what page, which, I don't know.

**Jessica** *moans loudly, an agonized exhalation that frightens* **Dali**.

**Dali**   Please.

**Freud**   It's all right.

**Dali**   To help me, please.

**Freud**   She's all right. She'll be all right.

*He takes the chair.*

Rebecca? Rebecca? What is wrong with your hand?

**Jessica**   The excrement.

**Freud**   Your breast?

**Jessica**   And my fingers; covered in shit. I know! I know! But I can't, it's ... I'm still so angry!!

**Freud**   Angry.

**Jessica**   Yes, angry.

**Freud**   At the bird?

*She breaks down. Gags.*

What is wrong with your mouth?

**Jessica**   The taste.

**Freud**   Describe the taste.

**Jessica**   The taste of salt. It's salt. Everything tastes of salt!! I'm filthy with this shit and all I can taste is salt.

**Freud**   Associate. The taste of salt.

**Jessica**   A candle burns upside down; its reflection in mahogany. The dinner party.

**Freud**    A candle?

**Jessica**    Put it out. No; the ... cutlery.

**Freud**    Tell me about the candle.

**Jessica**    It's in the middle of the dining table.

**Freud**    No, the other candle.

**Jessica**    What other? There is no other candle. Except the one I was allowed. I hate the dark; my mother allows me a candle. My father thinks it a waste. He will open my door and bark 'put it out'. The door opens ...

*Pause. She's still for a moment.*

Don't put the knife in your mouth. He opens the door. Put out the candle. The taste of salt and my ... my fingers.

*She sobs quietly.*

**Freud**    Why are you crying?

**Jessica**    I don't know.

**Freud**    I think you know. The candle is burning.

*Sobbing openly, growing in violence.*

**Jessica**    The candle is burning. He opens the door. He says 'put it out.' Put it ...! Put it ...!

**Freud**    That's enough.

**Jessica**    The candle is not upside down! It's me, I'm upside down! My head is hanging over the side of the bed. Put it ...!

**Freud**    That's enough now. Rebecca.

**Jessica**    Put it in your mouth!!

*Incapable of continuing, she stops.*

**Freud**    Rebecca. No more now.

**Jessica**    She remembered. She remembered. The mess on

her breast and her fingers and the taste of salt.

**Dali**   Don't cry. Please.

**Jessica**   I'm sorry. I'll be all right in a minute.

**Dali**   What was this?

**Freud**   She had remembered being raped. Orally. Before she was five years old.

**Jessica**   The taste of salt was the taste of her father's semen. The filth on her breast that she tried to clean off was his. When she woke in the morning her fingers were stuck together. She had to be carried from your study, and accompanied home. She slept for almost three days.

**Freud**   Over the next few sessions she released a great deal of anger and began to examine her feelings of guilt. She regained her appetite and her physical symptoms disappeared.

**Jessica**   She was ecstatic. (*Reads.*) 'For the first time in my adult life I am happy. A simple thing to have been so painfully elusive. I feel there is nothing now in my past that can throw a shadow over my future. This morning I shall prepare . . . a picnic basket.'

**Freud**   However. The events that Rebecca had remembered . . .

**Jessica**   Miriam! Her name was Miriam.

**Dali**   And she and her husband?

**Jessica**   Oh, eventually. Sexual relations were resumed. Which I suppose means *I* also have you to thank, Professor Freud.

**Freud**   What for?

**Jessica**   My life.

**Freud**   She was your mother.

**Jessica**   You cured her.

**Freud**    You have her mouth.

**Jessica**    You released her, enabled her. You were her saviour.

**Dali**    Is good. You come not to criticize, but to pay homage.

**Jessica**    What did you think, Professor?

**Freud** *lowers his head, thinking.*

**Jessica**    When I found her journal I had to come.

**Dali**    I like this. Your mother is cured and is a happy ending, yes?

**Jessica**    Not really, no.

**Dali**    No?

**Jessica**    Nine years later my mother died in the washroom of an insane asylum near Paris. She took a rubber tube they used for giving enemas and swallowed it; force fed it to herself. The other end she attached to a faucet, turned the tap, and drowned. In case you're still wondering Professor, that is why I'm here.

# Act Two

*The same. Twilight.*

**Dali**   Is serious now, yes?

**Jessica**   Yes.

**Dali**   I go put my trousers on.

*He retires to the closet.*

**Freud**   I had no knowledge of your mother's death.

**Jessica**   That's hardly surprising. Rebecca S. has little in common with Miriam Stein. Your patient Rebecca is a successful case history; my mother Miriam a suicidal hysteric.

**Freud**   The last time I saw her was a year or so after our final session. She returned to inform me of her health and happiness.

**Jessica**   She was pregnant, with me.

**Freud**   She had had, she said, a wonderful year.

**Jessica**   1897.

**Freud**   What?

**Jessica**   1897.

**Freud**   But that would make you ... It was ...?

**Jessica**   1897.

*An air-raid siren sounds.*

What is that?

**Freud**   A warning, is all.

*Frightened,* **Jessica** *covers her head with her arms.*

To alert us, not harm us.

**Dali** *comes out of the closet, crosses and exits out the door.*

**Dali**   *Scuse.*

**Freud** *draws the curtains. The intercom buzzes.*

**Freud**   Yes?

**Anna** *(off)*   Father? We are going to the shelter.

**Freud**   I'm not. I told you when you built it.

**Anna** *(off)*   This might not be another drill.

**Freud**   I have been thrown out of my home, shunted over Europe, and shipped across the channel. No further.

**Anna** *(off)*   It's just down the garden. Fifty yards.

**Freud**   I shall soon be spending a substantial amount of time in a hole in the ground. I don't intend to climb into one while I can still argue the point.

**Anna** *(off)*   Very well. But keep the curtains closed.

**Freud**   Of course.

**Anna** *(off)*   And if there are bombs, get under the desk.

**Freud**   Don't be absurd.

*He switches it off.* **Dali** *enters in a gas mask.*

**Dali**   *Scuse.*

*And goes back into the closet.*

**Freud**   If you would prefer to shelter . . .

**Jessica**   No. I would prefer to talk.

**Freud**   What were you looking for last night?

**Jessica**   Unpublished notes. Relevant material. I wanted to find out if you knew what you did to her?

**Freud**   I?

**Jessica**   On that final visit.

**Freud** She was strong, healthy, and functioning well.

**Jessica** Obviously you *had* managed to turn her into a horse.

**Freud** Her symptoms had subsided, her neuroses were negligible.

**Jessica** And my father could penetrate her whenever he so desired. Thank you doctor; my wife is cured.

**Freud** Not cured no, rendered capable. Remarkably so, considering.

**Jessica** What?

**Freud** That her analysis was incomplete.

**Jessica** Was it? Was it?

*Jessica takes a book from the shelf. Opens it at a page she's previously marked.*

**Jessica** The Aetiology of Hysteria. 1896. 'In every case the cause of hysteria is a passive sexual experience before puberty, ie, a traumatic seduction.' This is what you wrote.

**Freud** Yes it is.

**Jessica** No equivocation, no trace of doubt. You wrote to your friend Fliess; 'Have I revealed the great clinical truth to you? Hysteria is the consequence of pre-sexual shock.' That's what you believed.

**Freud** Yes it is.

**Jessica** And you published.

**Freud** Yes I did.

**Jessica** You were absolutely certain.

**Freud** Yes I was.

*She pulls a crumpled letter from a wellington boot.*

**Jessica** One year later. 'My Dear Fliess. Let me tell you

straight away the great secret which has been slowly
dawning on me in recent months. I no longer believe in
my neurotica.'

**Freud** What is the point you wish to make?

**Jessica** Just one year later. And you what, you . . .

**Freud** A year?

**Jessica** Change your mind in less than a . . .

**Freud** The year of my life! 1897 may have been a
wonderful year for your mother, but it was torture for me.

**Jessica** Why?

**Freud** My clinical cases. I suffered disappointment after
disappointment; the analyses refused to come to a
satisfactory conclusion; the results were imperfect
therapeutically and scientifically. I came to the inevitable
conclusion that I was wrong.

**Jessica** And when my mother returned, smiling, to
confide her happiness and my genesis to you . . . you took
back your blessing.

**Freud** At first I believed I had uncovered the inciting
trauma. A year later I knew this was not the case.

**Jessica** You told my mother that her memory of abuse
was a fantasy born of desire.

**Freud** It is more complex than that.

**Jessica** It's not that complex, Professor. You said her
father did not seduce her; that it was she who wished to
seduce her father.

**Freud** That is a gross over-simplification.

**Jessica** But by the autumn of that year, all the childhood
seductions unearthed by your patients; none of them had
ever occurred.

**Freud** In the unconscious there is no criterion of reality.

Truth cannot be distinguished from emotional fiction.

**Jessica**   So you abandoned them.

**Freud**   I abandoned the theory. It was false and erroneous.

**Jessica**   I don't have many vivid memories of my mother. She never went out, and she ate alone. I never ate a single meal with her. She would have fits which terrified me. I don't remember her treating me badly, but nor do I have the faintest recollection of her loving me. My father had her committed when I was five years old. I never saw her again.

**Freud**   If we had the time I could help you understand . . .

**Jessica**   I understand perfectly. I've spent a long time working to understand this. When you proposed that abuse was the root cause of so much mental illness your movement was at its most vulnerable. You needed the support of the intelligentsia, of institutions, of publishers and instead you were laughed at and reviled. Doors were closed. Anti-Semitic tracts appeared. Everything you'd worked for was threatened.

**Freud**   True.

**Jessica**   Your patients were the daughters and wives of wealthy and privileged men. Whom you began to accuse of molesting their own children. And then suddenly, you decide you were wrong. How convenient.

**Freud**   Convenient? To have shared a revelation and then discover it was false? All I had to steer myself through that terrible year was my integrity.

**Jessica**   Huh.

**Freud**   I have weathered many storms of protest, but I have never bowed to outrage or to ignorance.

**Jessica**   Had you not changed your mind, the outraged

and ignorant would have crucified you!! My own
grandfather, who my mother accused, was friend or
acquaintance to every publisher in Austria!

**Freud**    You are accusing me of the most heinous
opportunism!

**Jessica**    Yes. Yes I am!

**Freud**    Do you realize how many women retrieved
'memories' of abuse while lying there?

**Jessica**    Many.

**Freud**    More than many. You will forgive my
astonishment at being asked to believe that sexual
perversion was prevalent amidst the genteel classes in
epidemic proportions. I was proposing a virtual plague of
perversion. Not merely socially unacceptable; fundamentally
unthinkable!

**Jessica**    So you thought up something else.

**Freud**    The theory of infantile sexuality . . .

**Jessica**    . . . Is the cornerstone of your entire edifice! Take
*that* idea away and psychoanalysis would be rubble.

**Freud**    No one has been readier than I to risk our
movement in the pursuit of truth.

**Jessica**    My mother . . .

**Freud** (*harsh*)    Your mother was an hysteric! Her memories
of seduction were wishful fantasies based on her
unconscious desire to possess her father, his penis and his
child.

**Jessica**    But my mother . . .

**Freud**    These desires in turn based on her desire to possess
her mother, to suckle indefinitely, and to give her a child.

**Jessica**    I've read all this . . .

**Freud** (*rapid*)    A premature rejection of her mother, an unresolved anger at having no penis, a fierce fixation on her father. At the crucial age of seven, if my memory serves me, her mother dies. She believes herself to be guilty of killing her mother to attain her father. Her development is arrested, her guilt repressed along with her desires. Years later she develops the hysterical symptoms and the fantasies begin to emerge alongside the memories.

**Jessica**   But it's all so . . .

**Freud**   Complex.

**Jessica**   All I know is that my mother's father . . .

**Freud**   You know nothing!! You are ignorant, presumptuous and obsessed. Your theories are simplistic. Your motives malicious. I have given you quite enough of my time. Thank you.

**Jessica**   Why so angry?

**Freud**   I AM ANGRY WITH NO ONE!!

**Dali** (*off*)   Arrgh!

*He bursts out of the cupboard, holding his forefinger before him like a beacon. It's bleeding.*

**Dali**   Maphu mothur ufgud! Haffmee!

*He tears off his gas mask.*

**Dali**   Is my blood.

**Jessica**   What have you done?

**Dali**   Please, call an ambulance and alert the hospital. Look, is my blood. Is coming out of my finger.

**Jessica**   Calm down, it's not that bad.

**Dali**   Is my blood.

**Jessica**   Have you first aid?

**Freud**   In the drawer. How did you cut yourself?

**Dali**  Is not! I sit in the closet, I notice on the wall the
piece of ... how you say this? Nasal mucus. Fastened to
the wall with much exhibitionism. Very old; a previous
owner I am sure. Is pearly green with a sharp point that
makes a gesture which is a trumpet call for intervention. Is
disgusting, so I take my courage, wrap my finger in
handkerchief and savagely tear the mucus from the wall!
But is hard and steely point like a needle! Look; is here. It
penetrate between the nail and the flesh! All the way down.

**Jessica**  All right, calm down.

**Dali**  Is great painful.

**Jessica**  I'm sure it is.

**Dali**  Is to the bone.

**Jessica**  I'll pull it out.

**Dali**  Please. Be carefully.

*She pulls out the mucus. Wraps it in handkerchief.*

Argh!

**Jessica**  Here; disinfect it with this.

**Dali**  Is throbbing.

**Jessica**  Be a brave soldier.

**Freud** *begins reading his letters to Fliess.*

**Dali**  Is go boom boom boom; the music of perfidious
infection. Argh!

**Jessica**  What?

**Dali**  Is still there! The pointy part is still deep down. I
see it through the nail. Get it out.

**Jessica**  Well, I can't.

**Dali**  Do this!

**Jessica**  It's far too deep.

**Dali**  No! Is, but . . . ! Is still throb. Is will be infected. Is death. Death weigh in my hand like ignominous kilo of gesticulating worms.

**Jessica**  It's only a splinter.

**Dali**  Is unknown nasal mucus! This finger is swelled. This hand is begin to rot. Please, get me to a hospital. I have it surgically dismissed at the wrist. Buried. It decompose without me.

**Jessica**  It's not snot anyway.

**Dali**  It's not?

**Jessica**  No, it's not.

**Dali**  *Si si*! It's snot. Is what I said.

**Jessica**  It's a bit of glue.

**Dali**  It's not.

**Jessica**  No. A drop of wood glue.

**Dali**  Oh. *Si.*

**Jessica**  You'll survive.

**Dali**  Is possible. Thank you.

**Freud** *replacing letters in cabinet.*

**Jessica**  What are you doing?

**Freud**  I'm sorry?

**Jessica**  I haven't read them all yet.

**Freud**  And why should I allow you to examine my personal correspondence?

**Jessica**  Why should you not?

**Freud**  Because it is personal. The discovery of your mother's sad history has been very traumatic for you, but whatever quest you have set yourself is a hopeless one. I have nothing to hide.

*Loud knocks from the front door.*

Who the devil? Indeed, to hide nothing has been my sole quest.

*He leaves, taking the letters with him.*

**Jessica**    Then let me read those letters!

**Freud** (*off*)    Certainly not!

**Yahuda**'s *voice off, then both enter.*

**Yahuda**    Freud. Apologies for this but I must beg hospitality. Every time I turn on my bicycle lamp I'm yelled at by cockney plebeians in flat caps and armbands. It's pitch black; I can't get home. Ah.

**Freud**    Nor can Mr Dali and his wife.

**Dali** *looks for his wife.*

Your wife.

**Dali**    Please?

**Yahuda**    We met earlier.

**Dali**    Oh, *si. Si.*

**Yahuda**    How's the training going? Both pretty fit?

**Dali**    Which is this?

**Yahuda**    I got on top of one or two myself when I was younger.

**Dali**    Please?

**Yahuda**    Couldn't keep it up though.

**Dali**    Oh, *si.*

**Yahuda**    The nice thing is they don't have to be enormous to be satisfying, wouldn't you agree? If you're not used to it small ones are quite sufficiently stimulating. How far up her do you hope to get?

**Dali**    This man is a doctor?

**Freud**    I mentioned that you and your wife . . .

**Yahuda**    A word of advice; always use the best quality rope and don't attempt anything vertical the first time.

**Dali**    Please?

**Freud**    That you and your wife much enjoyed mountaineering.

**Dali**    Oh?

**Jessica**    I think it's time Dr Yahuda was told the truth.

**Freud**    No.

**Jessica**    Mr Dali and I are not married.

**Freud**    But share a common law agreement. It's a changing world, Yahuda.

**Jessica**    We met for the first time earlier this afternoon.

**Freud**    A rapidly changing world.

**Yahuda**    So why were you here in the first place?

**Jessica**    It is true that I am Russian.

**Freud**    Is it? Good.

**Jessica**    And I have been engaged by Professor Doctor Freud to translate some of his letters.

**Freud**    Yes, that's it. Precisely.

**Jessica**    And those are the only ones I haven't done.

**Freud**    Ah.

**Jessica**    May I continue?

**Freud**    No.

**Jessica**    Why not?

**Yahuda**    Why not?

**Freud**    Very well. If you must.

**Jessica** *takes the letters.* **Freud** *can't let go of them. She pulls, third time lucky.*

**Jessica**    Thank you, Professor.

*She retires to read.*

**Yahuda**    What's wrong with your hand?

**Freud**    Nothing. Hysterical grip reflex. When I was young I er . . .

*Makes a repeated gesture with his wrist. Recognizes it as an obscene gesture.*

. . . dropped an icecream.

**Yahuda** *finds the manila envelope containing the Moses article.*

**Yahuda**    Stamped and addressed, I see. Off to the publisher's?

**Freud**    Yes.

**Yahuda**    You realize of course, you have a Moses complex?

**Freud**    I beg your pardon?

**Yahuda**    I read an article. Some woman you once sent barmy. Said you identified with Moses.

**Freud**    Moses is nothing but the flesh of sublimation.

**Dali**    Superb.

*He makes a note.*

**Yahuda**    It is a bad time to discourage men from putting their faith in God.

**Freud**    On the contrary.

**Yahuda**    Have you read this evening's paper?

**Freud**    No.

**Yahuda**    Then do so.

*Slaps it at him.*

Seven thousand Jewish shops looted. Three hundred synagogues burned to the ground. Babies held up to watch Jews being beaten senseless with lead piping. They are calling it *Kristallnacht.*

**Freud** *takes the paper.*

**Yahuda**    Apparently Goering is displeased that so much replacement glass will have to be imported. He said they should have broken less glass and killed more Jews. Have you heard from your sisters?

**Freud**    No.

**Jessica**    Sisters?

**Freud**    Four elderly ladies. We have not been successful in our attempts to bring them out.

**Yahuda**    Don't blame yourself.

**Freud**    It is entirely my fault.

**Yahuda**    No.

**Freud**    If I myself had left sooner, I would have been more able to make suitable arrangements.

**Yahuda**    You've done what you can.

**Freud**    I do not believe I shall see them again.

**Yahuda**    They say it is to be the last war. Do you think so?

**Freud**    My last.

**Yahuda**    You lead us from the wilderness and then abandon us. If you think you're Moses why for the love of God throw doubt upon him now?

**Jessica**    Why indeed?

**Freud**   Have you finished with those?

**Jessica**   It couldn't mean you wish to be doubted, could it?

**Freud**   I wish to be left in peace!

**Jessica**   You doubt nothing?

**Freud**   Nothing!

**Yahuda**   What are you reading?

**Freud**   Nothing.

**Jessica**   You should read them also.

**Freud**   Yahuda; a cigar?

**Yahuda**   You stink of cigars.

**Freud**   No more lectures, please. I have already smoked myself to death. I now do it purely for pleasure.

**Freud** *lights a cigar.*

**Jessica**   This one's interesting.

**Yahuda**   Is it?

**Freud**   No, it isn't. Yahuda, come with me. I need some fresh air.

**Yahuda**   What about the Luftwaffe?

**Freud**   You think from two thousand feet they could spot the butt of an old cigar?

**Yahuda**   With my luck they'll recognize you instantly.

**Yahuda** *and* **Freud** *exit into garden.*

**Dali**   What are you looking for?

**Jessica**   I don't know, but I think he does.

**Dali**   Please. Lift your arm. You owe this.

*She lifts her arm. He draws while she continues reading.*

**Dali**   Later, you and I; we have dinner of seafood. Crush the complacent shell of crab and lobster and eat the flesh while still surprised. Then, break into National Gallery and visit the London Exhibition of Degenerate Art courtesy of Adolph Hitler, then tomorrow at dawn, by the light of the sun rising over Primrose Hill I shall render your armpit through my eyes and into history.

**Jessica**   I'm washing my hair.

**Dali**   Heaven, to Dali, is the depilated armpit of a woman.

**Jessica**   Forget it. That's the hair I'm washing. Do you expect to make love to all your models?

**Dali**   Never. Sometimes they make love to one another, but Dali only watches.

**Jessica**   Is that honourable or sad?

**Dali**   Please, do not try to understand Dali. This is only his job, and believe me, is too difficult.

**Jessica**   You don't like being touched do you? I noticed earlier. It makes you anxious. It makes you squirm.

**Dali**   Please.

**Jessica**   Do you make love to your wife?

**Dali**   We did this, but no more.

**Jessica**   Why not?

**Dali**   The last time we made love, Dali, at the climax of his passion, cried out the name of another.

**Jessica**   Your mistress?

**Dali**   No, my own. Gala she say is over, and goes fuck fishermen.

**Jessica**   Does that bother you?

**Dali**   Gala I adore. She is everything. But no, I cannot let her to touch me. Always, I hate to be touched.

**Jessica**  So have I.

**Dali**  Is true?

**Jessica**  Unlike you I find it very painful.

**Dali**  Touching?

**Jessica**  Not touching. I pray I shall not have to live my entire life like this.

*He stands, she stiffens, he sits again. She stands and sits beside him. Their hands rise, fall, courting. Finally they hold hands for about four seconds, then let go.*

**Dali**  How was it for you?

**Jessica**  Wonderful, thank you.

*She moves away, wiping her hand.*

**Dali**  You feel the bones too? Is enough sex for Dali. How these ugly millions do this thing to get these gruesome children, all this sucking and prodding and body fluids in and out of one another I will never understand. Inside a beautiful woman is always the putrefying corpse of Dali's passion.

**Freud** *returns.*

**Freud**  Are you finished?

**Jessica**  No. Where's your friend?

**Freud**  He wished to be left alone. He is a good and powerful man. It is hard to see him powerless.

**Jessica**  It is hard to believe in good and powerful men, it is so often a contradiction in terms.

**Freud**  Give me the letters.

**Jessica**  No.

*She leaps up and goes into the closet. Pops out again.*

You regret nothing?

**Freud**   Nothing! In my life. Nothing! Except perhaps one inadvisable evening at *Rookery Nook*.

**Jessica**   Don't worry, I shan't be in here forever.

*Closes and locks the door behind her.*

**Freud**   Then come out for pity's sake! Say what you have to say and leave me alone! Is this me?

**Dali**   No. Is a drawing by Dali.

**Freud**   But is this what I look like?

**Dali**   To Dali, *si*.

**Freud**   I look dead.

**Dali**   Is no offence. Dali sees beneath.

**Freud**   Soon, then.

**Dali**   But before you go. Please. One thing you do for him.

**Freud**   What?

**Dali**   To judge the work of Dali. The world is a whore, there is no one can tell me. Only you.

**Freud**   Your work?

**Dali**   Please. You see, if this is no good in your eyes ... I have wasted the time of my life. When you look at my paintings, what do you see? Well, you see what I see, obviously, that is the point. But have I caught what we are chasing, you and I? Can you *see* the unconscious?

**Freud**   Oh, Mr Dali. When I look at a Rembrandt, or a classical landscape or a still life by Vermeer, I see a world of unconscious activity. A fountain of hidden dreams.

**Dali**   *Si?*

**Freud**   But when I look at your work I'm afraid all I see

is what is conscious. Your ideas, your conceit, your
meticulous technique. The conscious rendition of conscious
thoughts.

**Dali**   Then this ... He ... I see.

**Freud**   You murder dreams. You understand?

**Dali**   Of course. (*Pause.*) Of course.

**Freud**   I hope I've not offended you.

**Dali**   No, no no. Is just the Death of the Surrealist
Movement, is all.

**Freud**   Surely not.

**Dali**   Is no matter, but is caput. You tell me nothing I do
not know already. I shall give up the paint.

**Freud**   Oh please, not on account of me.

**Dali**   No, no no ...

**Freud**   You must continue.

**Dali**   No. No no no. No. All right, I shall continue. You
and me, we know is shit. But the world is a whore, she will
buy the shit. I shall buy a small island.

**Freud**   Could you spend your life pursuing something you
no longer believed in?

**Dali**   Oh yes, no problem.

**Jessica** *emerges from the closet.*

**Freud** *is now genuinely frightened of her.*

**Jessica**   I'm ready. I have it now. 1897. Who can tell me
what is odd about this sentence? 'Those guilty of these
infantile seductions are nursemaids, governesses, and
domestic servants. Teachers are also involved, as are
siblings.' Well?

**Dali**   Give us a clue.

**Jessica**   If you like.

*She finds another letter.*

**Jessica**   'The old man died on the night of October 23rd, and we buried him yesterday.' This was your father. 'He bore himself bravely, like the remarkable man that he was. By one of the obscure routes behind my consciousness his death has affected me deeply. By the time he died his life had been long over, but at death the whole past stirs within one.'

**Freud**   Give them to me.

**Jessica**   No. Nursemaids, governesses, servants, siblings . . . no mention of fathers, Professor?

**Freud**   I've had enough of your inquisitory meanderings.

**Jessica**   I need look no further! I know why you changed your mind. Another letter to Fliess, justifying your decision. Pleading your seduction theory could not stand up because 'In every case of hysteria the father, *not even excluding my own*, had to be blamed as a pervert'. Not even excluding my own!

**Freud**   My father was a warm-hearted man possessed of deep wisdom.

**Jessica**   And?

**Freud**   I loved and respected him.

**Jessica**   And.

**Freud**   This is preposterous.

**Jessica**   An earlier letter. 'I have now to admit that I have identified signs of psychoneuroses in Marie'. Who was Marie? Marie was your sister.

**Freud**   The error into which I fell was a bottomless pit which could have swallowed us all.

**Jessica**   Perhaps it should have done. You suspected your father.

**Freud**  That is quite enough.

**Jessica**  Your family leave for the summer, you stay alone. You embark on your own self-analysis.

*She flicks pages.*

**Freud**  Those letters are private.

**Jessica**  Analyse this sentence, Professor Freud. 'Not long ago I dreamt that I was feeling over-affectionate towards Matilde (my eldest daughter, aged nine) but her name was Hella and I saw the word Hella in heavy type before me.' I looked up the name. Hella means Holy. You desired that which was holy to you.

**Dali**  No. No more. This is a great man. It take one to know one, which is proof.

**Jessica**  Your mind was in turmoil! The year your father died you found him condemned out of your own mouth. And then you realized your own potential for complicity in such things. Your own daughter.

**Freud**  There was no desire. The dream fulfilled my wish to pin down a father as the originator of neurosis.

**Jessica**  Then you admit you suspected . . .

**Freud**  My *wish* to do so!

**Jessica**  And yet the year of his death . . .

**Freud**  I suspected nothing.

**Jessica**  The year of your own analysis . . .

**Freud**  Do not presume . . .

**Jessica**  You choose to denounce your own theories!

**Freud**  I had no choice!

**Jessica**  Other than denounce your own father! Other than denounce yourself!

**Dali**   No! You, miss-prissy-kiss-my-armpit-tightarsed-girlie say this slanderous things no more!

**Jessica**   It only remains for me to make my findings known.

**Freud**   To whom?

**Jessica**   I believe Dr Yahuda may lend a sympathetic ear.

*She exits into the garden.*

**Freud**   Come back here!

**Jessica**   Dr Yahuda!

**Dali**   She is cast aspersions on integrity of all great men!

**Freud**   Stop her. Bring me those letters.

**Dali**   She is need have her head examined!

**Dali** *pursues.* **Yahuda** *enters through the DS door.*

**Yahuda**   I've mislaid my gas mask. Did I leave it in here?

**Freud**   I've not seen it.

**Yahuda**   Maybe on the porch.

**Freud**   No. I think I saw it in the hall.

**Yahuda**   I've looked in the hall.

**Freud**   I'll look with you.

*The sound of breaking glass.*

**Yahuda**   What's that?

**Freud**   Nothing. I'm not sure. Probably just a . . . bomb.

**Yahuda**   A bomb!?

**Freud**   Very likely.

**Yahuda**   But it's just a drill.

**Freud**   Unexploded. So far. I suggest we take immediate

refuge.

**Yahuda**  In the shelter?

**Freud**  No! Under the stairs.

**Yahuda**  Under the what?

**Freud** *hustles* **Yahuda** *out the door.* **Jessica** *enters through the window. Scrunching through broken glass off.*

**Dali** (*off*)  You think it discourage Dali you wield at him the greenhouse? No! Scabrous little non-fornicating fantasists like you Dali will squeezed between his fingernails!

*She notices the buff envelope on the desk. An idea comes to her. She removes the 'Moses and Monotheism' text from the envelope and puts the Fliess letters in its place, resealing the envelope.*

*The other text she puts in the maroon file.*

You must learn to respect for betters and olders and men who struggle in the mind like a silly girl could not begin to do!

*As she finishes he bursts in holding a length of hemp rope.*

Is swing, from tree. You want to give me papers and shut up and be good girl, or I do this worst thing to you.

*She picks up a phallic stone figure.*

**Jessica**  Try it.

**Dali**  What a woman. Is heavy, no?

**Jessica**  Yes.

**Dali**  So. I am fearless, *sí?*

*He takes a step forward, she swings the figure, he cowers.*

**Dali**  Donta hita the head! Is full of precious stuff!

*Enter* **Freud**.

**Freud**  Move the U-bank and tuck yourself well in.

**Yahuda** (*off*)   This is absurd.

**Freud**   I'll find your mask.

*Closes the door behind him.*

**Dali**   Dali is got her but she grow violent, so best cure her quickly, *si*?

**Jessica**   There's nothing wrong with me.

**Dali**   Put this down or be warned.

**Jessica**   Go to hell.

**Dali**   OK. OK. You push Dali to employ his superior intellect!

*He picks up a similar but much larger figure.*

**Freud**   That phallus is four thousand years old!

**Jessica**   What about this one?

*She throws hers at* **Dali**.

**Freud**   Catch it!

**Dali** *catches it but drops his own weapon on his foot.*

**Dali**   Got it. Argh!

**Jessica** *runs out of the French windows.*

**Jessica**   Dr Yahuda!

**Dali**   All right, now is personal.

*He pursues her, taking a really big figure.* **Freud** *picks up the maroon file and goes to the filing cabinet.*

**Freud** *changes his mind, crosses to the stove, opens the lid, and drops the file in the fire. The fire roars.*

**Yahuda** *enters.*

**Yahuda**   What do you want?

**Freud**   Nothing.

**Yahuda**  Not you; her.

**Freud**  Who?

**Yahuda**  I heard shouts.

**Freud**  For the warden. There is a large unexploded bomb in the greenhouse.

**Jessica** *(off)*  I need your help, Yah . . . *(Hand clamped over her mouth.)* . . . huda!

**Yahuda**  There, you see?

**Freud**  No, no. Our local warden is Mr Yahoohaa.

**Jessica** *(off)*  Yahuda!

**Yahuda**  I distinctly heard my name.

**Freud**  Nonsense. It's all in my head. Your head.

**Yahuda**  Was that a Freudian slip?

**Freud**  Certainly not.

*He trips over the rug.*

Excuse me. I must . . . the bomb.

*He picks up a soda siphon and exits into the garden.* **Yahuda** *spots the buff envelope and picks it up. Unable to restrain himself, he takes it to the stove and hesitates.*

**Jessica** *(off)*  Dr Yahuda!

*This spurs him to action. He lifts the lid.*

**Jessica** *enters, her head bleeding, and tied round the waist by a rope. On the end of the rope, attempting to restrain her,* **Freud** *and* **Dali**.

**Jessica**  Oh, thank Go . . . no! Don't do that!!

**Yahuda**  I was er . . . warming my hands!

**Jessica**  What's that envelope doing in them?

**Yahuda**  Good grief; thank God you spotted that.

**Freud**   How dare you!

*He takes the envelope from him.*

**Freud**   Have you no regard for a man's life's work?

**Yahuda**   Life's work? Senile piffle.

**Jessica**   There's something you must know. The theory of infantile sexuality is based upon . . . (a false premise!)

**Freud** *puts a gas mask on her.*

**Freud**   This woman has turned violently psychotic.

*She yells her findings unintelligibly.*

**Freud**   In extreme cases I'm afraid only extreme methods will suffice.

**Jessica** *tries her best.*

**Freud**   You see; senseless ramblings.

**Dali**   Please to calm down like the good little girl should be seen and not heard.

*She gives up.*

**Freud**   But you Yahuda; you should be ashamed of yourself. A man's words are his legacy. They should not be censored, but should stand in their entirety . . .

*Checks the contents.*

**Freud**   . . . aahg! No, you're right, let's burn the damn stuff.

**Yahuda**   Bravo!

**Jessica**   No!

*She grabs it.* **Dali** *tries to get it off her.*

**Dali**   Leave this things alone now; is none of little girls' business.

**Freud**   Give it to me!

**Jessica**   Yahuda . . . read this.

*She gives the envelope to* **Yahuda***.*

**Yahuda**   What?

**Jessica**   Read it. Read it!

**Yahuda**   I've already read it.

**Freud** *takes the envelope and manages to secure it in a drawer.*

**Freud**   It has been a very stimulating afternoon, but I must ask you all to leave now.

**Freud** *goes for the door. He pulls the handle, but the door has become rubber-like. It bends without opening.*

**Freud**   Good God.

**Dali**   How you do this?

**Freud**   What's going on.

**Dali**   Do it again.

**Jessica**   Don't let him destroy the letters.

**Yahuda**   What?

**Jessica**   The envelope; don't let him burn it.

**Freud** *uses the intercom.*

**Freud**   Anna!

**Dali** *tries the door.*

**Dali**   Is fantastic.

**Freud**   Anna!

*From the intercom a* **Child***'s scream.*

**Child**   No, Papa! No!

*And a* **Father***'s solemn reprimand.*

**Father**   Sigmund.

**Freud**    No.

*Turns off the intercom and retreats in fright.*

**Yahuda**    What was that?

**Freud**    Nothing. You heard it?

**Jessica**    I will not be silenced.

**Freud**    You will leave this house.

**Jessica**    I shall go to the papers.

**Freud**    I shall call the police.

**Jessica**    I shall publish the letters.

**Freud** *picks up the phone. It turns into a lobster.*

**Freud**    Hello? Would you please connect me with ...
aaaargh!

**Yahuda**    What the hell is going on here?

**Dali**    Don't look at me.

**Freud**, *frightened now, goes for the door, thinks better of it, heads
for the French windows.*

**Freud**    Everything's fine. But reluctantly I must bring the
evening to a close.

*He opens the curtains. A train is hurtling across the garden towards
him. Steam, bright lights glaring straight ahead, and a piercing
whistle.*

**Freud**    Arrgh!

**Yahuda**    What the devil?

**Freud** *closes the curtains.*

**Yahuda**    What was that?

*The clock strikes.* **Freud**, *terrified, compares his watch. The clock
melts.*

**Yahuda**    What's happening?

**Dali**    Is the camembert of time and space, no?

*A deep dangerous, thunderous music begins, low at first, building. The edges of the room begin to soften.*

**Jessica**    Doctor Yahuda, you have to hear me, before it's too late.

**Freud**    No!

**Yahuda**    Are you all right?

**Freud**    Please Yahuda . . .

**Yahuda**    You look unwell.

**Freud**    Go home.

**Yahuda**    I'm your physician Freud, not another figment of your addled imagination.

**Freud**    But if you were it would please me most to imagine you sitting by the fire with a good book . . . *at home.*

**Yahuda** *disappears through a trap door, or in a puff of pantomime smoke.*

**Jessica** *gets a hand free and tears off the mask.*

**Jessica**    Dr Yahuda!

**Freud**    Gone! Ha ha!

**Jessica**    Then I shall go too. And find someone willing to listen.

**Freud**    No. No. I'm getting the hang of this now. You are nothing more than a neurotic manifestation . . .

**Jessica**    Of what?

**Freud**    Of a buried subconscious . . . of a . . .

**Jessica**    What?

**Freud**    You don't exist. I can't hear you.

**Jessica**   Of a what?

**Freud**   The vaguest sense ...

**Jessica**   Of what?

**Freud**   Of g ... Get out of my head! House!! Head!!!

*The room continues to melt.*

**Dali**   Back in the closet and there to stay.

**Jessica**   Let me go!

*She kicks* **Dali** *in the crotch and dashes out of the down stage door. He dives for and catches the rope.*

**Dali**   Is no panic. He is got her!

*Her momentum pulls him out of the room.*

**Freud**   And stay out.

*But* **Dali** *reappears almost instantly, pulling the rope.*

**Dali**   Is OK. She not got anywhere.

**Freud**   Let her go.

**Dali**   I bring her back.

**Freud**   No!

**Dali**   Is no problem.

**Freud**   Just ... let the rope go.

**Dali**   You and me we sort this women out once and for all, *sí?*

**Freud**   No, please ...

**Dali**   Come back here you hysterical bitch!

**Freud**   Please, don't ... !

**Dali** *gives an almighty tug.* **Jessica** *is no longer tied to the rope. Into the room spills a nude* **Woman**. *Glittering music.*

**Freud**   No.

**Dali**    Who is this?

**Freud**    No, please . . .

*The* **Woman** *moves towards* **Freud***; he's both attracted and repelled.*

**Dali**    Is fantastic! But is who?

**Freud**    Matilde?

**Woman**    Papa.

**Freud**    No. Matilde?

*The* **Woman** *embraces* **Freud***.*

**Woman**    Papa.

**Freud**    Oh, my Matilde . . .

*The embrace turns sexual.*

**Freud**    No.

**Dali**    Is the most desirable, no?

**Freud**    No! Don't touch me.

*He disengages.*

**Freud**    I never . . . ! I never even imagined . . . !

**Woman**    Papa!

**Freud**    Leave me alone!

*He runs to the window. She pursues him. A train whistle blows in the garden, and the curtains billow.* **Freud** *backs away from the window. The* **Woman** *tries to embrace him. He avoids her and runs to hide in the closet. Opens the door and through it topples a cadaverous, festering, half-man, half-***Corpse***. Screeching music.*

Ahhh!

**Dali**    Aaaargh!

**Corpse**    Sigmund!

**Freud**   Gold help me.

*The* **Corpse** *pursues* **Freud**. *The* **Woman** *tries to embrace him.* **Dali**, *in terror, climbs on to the filing cabinet.*

**Woman**   Papa.

**Corpse**   Sigmund!

*Sounds of shunting trains compete with music; a drowning cacophony. Grotesque* **Images** *appear, reminiscent of* **Dali**'s *work, but relevant to* **Freud**'s *doubts, fears and guilts.* **Freud** *is horrified as the contents of his unconscious are spilled across the stage.*

*More* **Bodies** *appear, reminiscent of concentration camp victims, as are the antique figures being scattered by the* **Woman** *and the* **Corpse**. *Distant chants from the Third Reich. Four* **Old Ladies** *appear.*

**Ladies**   Sigmund. Siggy. Sigmund.

*They make their way to a gas chamber. Heads hung, they undress . . .*

**Dali** *is hit by a swan.* **Freud** *moves to the door but it is suddenly filled by a huge, crippled, faceless* **Patriarch**. *He enters and towers over* **Freud**. *Music descends to a rumble.*

**Freud**   Papa?

**Jessica** (*off*)   Mama?

**Woman**   Papa?

**Jessica**   Mama?

**Corpse**   Sigmund!

*The* **Patriarch** *lifts his crutch and swings it, striking the cowering* **Freud** *a massive blow on the jaw.* **Freud** *screams in agony and collapses. The* **Patriarch** *pulls on the rope and* **Jessica** *finally spills into the room.*

**Jessica**   Mama? Mama? Mama?

*She is grasped and awkwardly embraced by the figure. Her eyes are screwed shut so as not to see his face.*

**Patriarch**    Open your eyes.

*She shakes her head.*

**Patriarch**    Open your eyes. Then I shall open them for you.

*The razor appears in his hand and he cuts open one of her eyes.*

**Patriarch**    Now, do you see?

*Music crashes. Lights crash to a tight downlight on* **Freud**. *Stillness. Silence.*

**Freud**    Deeper than cancer. The past. And of all the years, the year I looked into myself is the one that has been killing me. In the months of May and April, one by one, I hunted down my fears, and snared them. Throughout the summer, mounted, pinned and labelled each of them. In October; my anger, for the most part, I embalmed. And in December I dissected love. Love has ever since been grey and lifeless flesh to me. But there has been little pain. The past, for the most part, has passed. I chose to think, not feel.

**Dali** *leans into his light, smiles.*

**Dali**    Better now?

**Freud**    Am I dying?

**Dali**    *Si.*

**Freud**    And all this?

**Dali**    Don't blame me for this; is nothing to do with. I tell you already; surrealism is dead. Besides; is impossible to understand.

**Dali** *gestures. The* **Patriarch**, *the* **Woman**, *the* **Corpse** *and the* **Old Ladies** *all disappear. The set begins to return to normal.*

**Freud**    What about you?

**Dali**    Dali? Is true. He visit you. This was two months ago. And he look at the death in your face of Freud and

he understand how many things were at last to end in
Europe with the end of your life. But apart from this he
visit and ... nothing happens much.

**Freud**   Yahuda?

**Dali**   Many Jews.

**Freud**   Her?

**Dali**   She is nothing. Please.

**Dali** *sits* **Freud** *in his chair.*

**Dali**   So ... Dali visits. Freud remembers ... sleeps.
Goodnight.

*Exit* **Dali**.

*The air-raid all-clear siren sounds. The set completes its return to
normal, as do the lights.*

**Jessica** *stands looking at the sleeping* **Freud**.

**Jessica**   Professor?

*His eyes open.*

**Jessica**   Were you sleeping?

**Freud**   I don't believe so.

**Jessica**   I'm sorry I got angry.

**Freud**   To get angry is most necessary.

**Jessica**   Better out than in?

**Freud**   Certainly.

**Jessica**   But what about those who get hurt?

**Freud**   If the anger is appropriately expressed ...

**Jessica**   What about the children?

**Freud**   No one gets hurt.

**Jessica**   Ha?

**Freud**   It is painful to understand one's complicity in these things.

*Pause.*

**Jessica**   Do you still insist my mother was never molested by my grandfather?

**Freud**   No, she was not.

**Jessica**   Well, that's a remarkable thing.

**Freud**   Why?

**Jessica**   Because I was. And please don't suggest that I imagined this. He was no beloved, half-desired father to me. He was a wiry old man who smelt of beer and cheese and would limp to my bed and masturbate on me. Only once was it an unexpected thing. And once he whispered if I told my father, he would do worse to me with this.

*She shows the razor.*

My mother knew what he would do, if she were not there to listen for the door, the creaking stair. That's why she protested at being sent away. And so fierce and vehement her protest, sent away she surely was.

**Freud** *bows his head.*

What was it you remembered in your self-analysis, Professor? About your father?

**Freud**   What is more relevant is what I could not remember.

**Jessica**   Have you no feelings?

**Freud**   I chose to think. And if now I am not so much a man as a museum, and my compassion just another dulled exhibit, so be it. All I have done, what I've become ... was necessary. To set the people free.

**Jessica**   Dead already.

**Freud**   Oh, a few bats hang in the tower; fear. The odd

rat still scampers through the basement; guilt. Other than that the building is silent.

**Jessica**   Liar.

**Freud**   I hear nothing.

**Jessica**   You heard me.

**Freud**   Nothing.

**Jessica**   Listen harder.

**Freud** *breaks down. Weeps.*

**Jessica**   What? What is it?

**Freud**   The exhibits are screaming.

**Jessica**   Goodbye.

**Freud**   I don't know your name.

**Jessica**   Jessica.

**Freud**   God is looking.

**Jessica**   Goodbye.

**Freud**   Jessica. The young may speak what the old cannot bear to utter.

**Jessica**   Because I can articulate these things does not mean I am able to bear them.

*She leaves.* **Yahuda** *enters and examines the chessboard.* **Freud** *speaks with difficulty.*

**Freud**   Yahuda?

**Yahuda**   Freud?

**Freud**   You will remember you promised to help me when the time came. Well, it's torture now.

**Yahuda** *nods.*

**Yahuda**   Have you spoken to Anna?

**Freud**    She will understand.

**Yahuda** *nods. From his bag he takes a hypodermic, prepares it, and injects* **Freud** *with two centigrams of morphine.*

**Freud**    Thank you, my friend. In the drawer. There are some carbons . . .

**Yahuda**    Which, these?

**Freud**    To Fliess.

**Yahuda**    I have them.

**Freud**    The one on the top.

**Yahuda**    Yes?

**Freud**    Take a pen. A pen; use ink. From the word 'father'.

**Yahuda**    Yes?

**Freud**    Delete for me five words. 'Not even excluding my own.'

**Yahuda**    Done.

**Freud**    Illegible?

**Yahuda**    Gone.

**Freud**    Thank you.

*He closes his eyes. Grimaces.*

**Yahuda**    I shall repeat the dose in twelve hours' time. Two centigrams, a little more, whatever's called for. You may hallucinate. Don't be afraid.

*The grimace tightens, then the drug takes hold.*

**Freud**    Oh . . . heaven.

*And* **Freud**'s *face relaxes as he falls into a sleep which will become his last.*

**Yahuda** *dismisses a tear, takes a last move at the chessboard and* *leaves quietly.*

*The sound of rain beyond the window, and a subtle change of light.*

**Freud** *wakes. Looks at his watch.*

**Freud**   If you are waiting for me to break the silence you will be deeply disappointed. The silence is yours alone, and is far more eloquent than you might imagine.

*He turns in his chair and looks towards the couch. Frowns when he sees there is no one on it.*

**Jessica** *appears through the rain and stops outside the French windows. Her hair hangs dripping to her shoulders.*

*She taps on the glass.* **Freud** *looks at her. Closes his eyes, too tired to go through all this again, but knowing he may have to.*

**Jessica** *continues to tap as the lights fade.*

# Dead Funny

## Characters

**Eleanor**   *Thirty-nine. Attractive, middle-class, part-time teacher at an adult education centre. Married to Richard.*

**Richard**   *Thirty-six. Consultant obstetrician and this year's honorary chairman of the Dead Funny Society.*

**Brian**   *Fifty-nine. Cheerful, slightly camp, founder and vice-chairman of the Dead Funny Society.*

**Nick**   *Thirty-six. Secondary school teacher of sciences. Member of the society. Married to Lisa.*

**Lisa**   *Thirty-three. Ex-dancer. Housewife, mother and member of the society.*

## Setting

Eleanor and Richard's living room in north London, or any up-market area bordering on city suburbs. Nice furnishings, a view to the front door. Door to kitchen. Door to rest of house. Television with video. Hanging human skeleton. Medical model of human torso with detachable organs. Framed mementoes of dead comedians.

Those to whom this should be dedicated would probably prefer to remain anonymous. But they have my undying affection.

**Dead Funny** was premièred at the Hampstead Theatre, London on 27 January 1994 with the following cast:

| | |
|---|---|
| **Eleanor** | Zoë Wanamaker |
| **Richard** | David Haig |
| **Brian** | Niall Buggy |
| **Lisa** | Beatie Edney |
| **Nick** | Danny Webb |

*Directed by* Terry Johnson
*Designed by* Sue Plummer
*Lighting design by* Simon Opie
*Sound design by* John A Leonard

*Artistic Director, Hampstead Theatre* Jenny Topper

# Act One

## Scene One

**Eleanor** *sits, motionless. On the floor, scattered toys and the torso, its organs spilled.* **Richard** *enters.*

**Richard** One night only. Wimbledon Theatre. Sunday night. Norman Wisdom. Norman Wisdom.

**Eleanor** Lucky Wimbledon.

**Richard** One night only.

**Eleanor** Might have been a whole week.

**Richard** Mr Grimsdale!

**Eleanor** You got a ticket?

**Richard** I got twelve.

**Eleanor** Handy. When you fall asleep you can stretch out.

**Richard** Don't laugh at me, 'cos I'm a fool.

**Eleanor** *laughs, softly and ironically.*

**Richard** What are you doing?

**Eleanor** Not hoovering up that digestive biscuit.

**Richard** *finds the torso.*

**Richard** Bloody hell, Eleanor.

**Eleanor** What?

**Richard** This isn't a toy.

**Eleanor** It's fun to play with.

**Richard** I don't like it being touched.

**Eleanor** If you don't want it touched put it somewhere it can't be touched.

**Richard**   I've had this since my father died.

**Richard** *finds scattered organs, sits to replace them in torso.*

**Eleanor**   I know; I live with it. And that.

**Richard**   Don't start.

**Eleanor**   Well, isn't it about time they were given a decent burial? Couldn't you help them through the pearly soft hatch and up to attic heaven?

**Richard**   It's an antique.

**Eleanor**   No Richard, a chair is an antique. A porcelain doll is an antique. Some poor Victorian sod's fibula is not an antique. God, they give me the creeps.

**Richard**   What they give you is an uncomfortable sense of your own mortality.

**Eleanor**   I'll give you an uncomfortable sense of your own mortality one of these days. I'll give you a permanent bloody sense of your own mortality!

**Richard**   The heart's missing.

*Another ironic laugh from* **Eleanor**.

**Richard**   Jesus.

**Eleanor**   Do you realize how old I am?

*Pause.*

**Eleanor**   I'm three years older than you.

**Richard**   You know I can never . . .

**Eleanor**   You must.

**Richard**   Remember.

**Eleanor**   Everyone knows how old they are.

**Richard**   I'm . . . thirty-five.

**Eleanor**   Thirty-six.

**Richard**   Thirty-six.

**Eleanor**   Time just passes you by, doesn't it? While the rest of us get dragged along. It's a quarter to nine.

**Richard**   So what?

**Eleanor**   It is late, Richard.

**Richard**   Don't call me Richard.

**Eleanor**   That's your name.

**Richard**   I know, but I don't like you calling me it. Look, I went to a pub. I had a drink.

**Eleanor**   Why tonight?

**Richard**   Why not?

**Eleanor**   In case you've forgotten, which I don't think you have, it's Wednesday.

*She stands, hands him the heart of the torso, then gathers toys.*

**Richard**   I know.

**Eleanor**   Well then.

**Richard**   Well then what?

**Eleanor**   You know what!

**Richard**   This is broken. Look, he's bloody well broken it.

**Eleanor**   Then you shouldn't leave it lying around to get broken.

**Richard**   I didn't leave it lying around; I left it in a perfectly appropriate place.

**Eleanor**   I hate that word. Appropriate. You never stop using it.

**Richard**   Because it's often the most appropriate word, presumably.

**Eleanor**   And that one; presumably.

**Richard**   If my vocabulary annoys you so much, why do you insist on having these cryptic fucking conversations?

**Eleanor**   Presumably Richard, because I think it's appropriate to do so. Richard.

**Richard**   Don't try to be cleverer than you are.

**Eleanor**   This is deliberate, isn't it? You're picking a fight.

**Richard**   I've had a difficult day.

**Eleanor**   Putting stuff between us. Pushing me away.

**Richard**   I've just done five hysterectomies. I really don't need this.

**Eleanor**   What?

**Richard**   All this.

**Eleanor**   How were they?

**Richard**   What?

**Eleanor**   The hysterectomies.

**Richard**   What do you mean, how were they?

**Eleanor**   How were they?

**Richard**   Uncomplicated.

**Eleanor**   And the patients?

**Richard**   Unconscious.

**Eleanor**   Can you remember their names?

**Richard**   Whose names?

**Eleanor**   When you're up to your wrists in someone . . .

**Richard**   Eleanor . . .

**Eleanor**   Is she still . . . Jennifer Simpson or is it just offal and chops?

**Richard**  What's wrong with you?

**Eleanor**  What were their names? These unconscious women whose uncomplicated wombs you whipped out today. I want their names.

*Pause.*

**Eleanor**  You don't know, do you?

**Richard**  Of course I know.

**Eleanor**  Go on then; tell me their names.

**Richard**  Christ, you're in a mood.

**Eleanor**  I knew you didn't know them.

**Richard**  I know them.

**Eleanor**  You don't.

**Richard** *puts the broken heart in place and closes the torso.*

**Eleanor** *winds and sets an alarm clock.*

**Richard**  A drink would be nice.

**Eleanor**  I know you. You'll let it get later and later.

**Richard**  I haven't eaten.

**Eleanor**  That's all right, I haven't cooked. Any more excuses?

**Richard**  I've got a verruca.

**Eleanor**  Did you bring a note from home?

**Richard**  Eleanor.

**Eleanor**  What?

**Richard**  I'm not in the mood.

**Eleanor**  Well, you never will be. Will you? That's the point, isn't it?

**Richard**  It just doesn't feel right . . .

**Eleanor**   I know it doesn't feel right. If it felt right we wouldn't have to do this. It's only an hour of your precious life.

**Richard**   Every other evening.

**Eleanor**   Twice a week.

**Richard**   For how long?

**Eleanor**   That's up to you, isn't it?

**Richard**   If it was up to me we wouldn't be doing it. If it was up to me I'd be sitting with a meal in front of me watching television.

**Eleanor**   You're doing this deliberately.

**Richard**   Doing what?

**Eleanor**   Making me angry. Making it impossible.

**Richard**   Eleanor . . .

**Eleanor**   Why am I Eleanor all of a sudden? I've been Ellie for ten years and all of a sudden I'm Eleanor. I'm only Eleanor when you're being deliberately provocative.

**Richard**   Don't lose your temper.

**Eleanor**   And if you tell me not to then you think I will, don't you? Don't you!

**Richard**   I won't say another word.

**Eleanor**   Oh, that'll get her, won't it? A bit of martyred silence. That'll make her so bloody angry she'll forget what day it is! Won't she? That'd suit you, wouldn't it?

**Richard**   Yes, that's right, whatever you say.

**Eleanor**   Then stay very calm and agree with her and she'll hit the fucking ceiling!! I WILL NOT GET ANGRY WITH YOU, YOU MANIPULATIVE SOD!!!

**Richard**   Do you want to come on Sunday?

**Eleanor**   What?

**Richard**   Norman Wisdom?

*She takes a deep breath.*

**Richard**   Should I keep a ticket for you?

**Eleanor** *laughs dangerously. She gets a bottle of gin, a bottle of martini, and a glass. Pours a glug of each and drinks.*

**Richard**   I'm tired, that's all.

**Eleanor**   Hard fucking luck.

**Richard**   Please. Stop swearing.

**Eleanor** (*quietly*)   Pig-faced cunt.

**Richard**   I beg your pardon?

**Eleanor**   I called my headmistress that once, back in the days when I occasionally expressed myself.

**Richard**   Can I have one of those?

*She pours another.*

**Eleanor**   You think you're tired. I'm exhausted. It's been want want want all day.

**Richard**   Mmm?

**Eleanor**   The baby.

**Richard**   Oh.

**Eleanor**   Apparently this is the first time they've been out together since he was born. Lisa looks as if she hasn't slept for a month. I've only ever sat on sleeping babies before today; I'd no idea. He screamed from five o'clock 'til half past seven. Didn't want milk, didn't want cuddles, certainly didn't want me . . .

**Richard**   I don't envy them.

**Eleanor**   Incessant noise from one end and packets of poo from the other.

**Richard**  Vile.

**Eleanor**  Gorgeous.

*Drinks the martini herself.*

**Eleanor**  I'm thirty-nine.

**Richard**  I know.

*She massages his shoulders.*

**Richard**  What's this? Affection or instruction?

**Eleanor**  What does it feel like??

**Richard**  Like you doing what you've been told.

*Hits him.*

**Richard**  Ow.

**Eleanor**  I thought of that all by myself.

**Richard**  No physical contact without previous consent.

**Eleanor**  You asked for it.

**Richard**  I'll tell the headmistress.

**Eleanor**  I wish you'd take this seriously.

**Richard**  I can't take Miriam seriously.

**Eleanor**  Not her, us.

*She drinks, sits next to him.*

**Eleanor**  State the parameters.

**Richard**  What?

**Eleanor**  You know the procedure.

**Richard**  We both know the parameters.

**Eleanor**  Miriam said we should state them.

**Richard**  All right then, state them.

**Eleanor**  You state them.

**Richard**   I can't remember them.

**Eleanor**   One hour alone together. Say it.

**Richard**   One hour alone together.

**Eleanor**   This week we touch. But we may not have intercourse.

**Richard**   Fuck, she said.

**Eleanor**   We may not fuck.

**Richard**   Do you think she ever has?

**Eleanor**   Who?

**Richard**   Miriam. I can't imagine it. Make love to Miriam, you might never be seen again.

**Eleanor**   Please concentrate.

**Richard**   We may not fuck. We may touch.

**Eleanor**   How may we touch?

**Richard**   We may touch each other anywhere but the genitals.

**Eleanor**   No.

**Richard**   No?

**Eleanor**   That was last week.

**Richard**   And this week's something else, is it?

**Eleanor**   This week we may touch each other anywhere, but neither must feel it necessary to climax in the other's company.

**Richard**   Couldn't we just take up bunji-jumping?

**Eleanor**   That's next week. Would you like to undress me?

**Richard**   No thank you.

**Eleanor**   Would you like me to undress you? Richard?

**Richard**  At one of my birthday parties; seventh, eighth; my mother made us play a game called Marks and Spencers. We're stood in two long rows and my mother calls out shoe or sock or vest and the first team to get whatever it is into this cardboard box gets a point. I throw one of my sandals in, but I can't say I enjoy it much. There's all these mothers cheering us on and suddenly mine, in a frenzy of encouragement, rips my T-shirt off.

**Eleanor**  That was so long ago.

**Richard**  I'm left standing there, all thin arms and goose-pimples.

**Eleanor**  You should go to an analyst.

**Richard**  No, my mother should have gone to an analyst. Another time she and my father stole my trousers. We're playing around, Sunday afternoon, suddenly I'm standing in the middle of the carpet in my white cotton underpants. I desperately want my trousers and they won't give them to me.

**Eleanor**  You should tell someone all this.

**Richard**  There's nothing wrong with me.

**Eleanor**  Richard . . .

**Richard**  Don't call me Richard.

**Eleanor**  Sorry. Sweetheart. Darling. Love. You don't have to do anything you don't want to. Now get undressed.

*He undresses. She reciprocates.*

**Richard**  I've lost a button on this.

**Eleanor**  It's in the pot next to the wok.

*He hesitates.*

Would it help if I went upstairs and slipped into something extremely uncomfortable?

**Richard**  No thanks. You're fine as you are.

*He sits in his underpants. She flicks his underpants' elastic. He removes them.*

**Eleanor**   How do you feel?

**Richard**   Naked.

**Eleanor**   Why?

**Richard**   ?

**Eleanor**   I'm your wife.

**Richard**   I'm stark naked.

**Eleanor**   Or I'm supposed to be.

**Richard**   So what am I supposed to feel?

**Eleanor**   Just . . .

**Richard**   Ecstatic? ·

**Eleanor**   Try to relax.

**Richard**   I feel fat, that's what I feel.

**Eleanor**   You're not fat.

**Richard**   What's that then?

**Eleanor**   It's nice. I like it.

**Richard**   That apple falling on Newton's head is a myth, you know. I'll tell you how he discovered gravity; on his thirty-fourth birthday he got out of the bath and there it was.

**Eleanor**   I think you've got a lovely body.

**Richard**   You think I should do hen nights?

**Eleanor**   You're not quite a Chippendale, Richard, more Texas Homecare.

**Richard**   Can I put it away please?

**Eleanor**   Stop talking. Lie down. Relax.

*She massages him.*

**Richard**   This is your idea of an erotic encounter, is it?

**Eleanor**   Yes; if I was twenty-seven, on a beach in Jamaica. With someone else. Joke.

**Richard**   Ho ho.

**Eleanor**   Miriam said the crucial thing is to relax.

**Richard**   I'd lay good money Miriam's never even done it.

**Eleanor**   Close your eyes.

**Richard**   That's probably why she's a therapist. Figures sooner or later she'll get a patient who's desperate enough to proposition her.

**Eleanor**   Turn over.

**Richard**   Do I have to?

**Eleanor**   Please.

*He turns over.*

**Eleanor**   What would you like?

**Richard**   I'd like to get dressed.

**Eleanor**   No. Imagine you're on a beach somewhere.

**Richard**   I hate the beach.

**Eleanor**   Why?

**Richard**   Because they make you take your clothes off. Oh, just touch it, will you?

**Eleanor**   What?

**Richard**   You're going everywhere but. Just touch it.

**Eleanor**   Do you mind?

**Richard**   Phone Nick and Lisa. Get a few people round; let everyone take turns.

**Eleanor**   I'm supposed to be allowed to touch it.

**Richard**   Then will you touch it, for Christ's sake.

**Eleanor**   Oh, this is ridiculous.

**Richard**   I know it's ridiculous. I feel ridiculous.

*He starts dressing.*

**Eleanor**   No.

*He stops.*

**Richard**   Ellie, please.

**Eleanor**   Not yet. Lie down.

*He lies down.*

**Eleanor**   Close your eyes.

*He closes his eyes. She touches his penis. The doorbell rings.*

**Eleanor**   I don't believe it.

**Richard**   That was amazing.

**Eleanor**   I do not believe it.

**Richard**   How did you make it do that?

**Eleanor**   We don't have visitors. When was the last time we had a visitor?

*Bell rings again.*

**Richard**   That is incredible; you were nowhere near it that time.

*He starts getting dressed.*

**Eleanor**   Who is it?

**Richard**   How should I know?

**Eleanor**   You've invited someone over, haven't you?

**Richard**   No.

**Eleanor**   You scheming sod. It'll be one of the society with a newsletter proof under his arm. 'Hello Ellie, sorry to disturb you; is Richard in?'

**Richard**   Ellie . . .

**Eleanor**   It'll be Brian. That's who it'll be.

**Richard**   Hold on a minute . . . !

*He struggles to get dressed. She opens the door.*

**Brian**   Hello Ellie, sorry to disturb you; is Richard in?

**Eleanor**   Hello Brian. Come on through.

**Richard**   Hold on.

*Enter* **Brian**.

**Brian**   I thought about phoning but then I thought not. Oh. Hello Richard.

**Richard**   Hi, Brian.

**Brian**   Sorry, have I disturbed you?

**Richard**   No. No. I was just . . . um.

**Eleanor**   Getting dressed.

**Brian**   Right you are. As one does.

**Eleanor**   He gets home from work Brian and he can't keep his hands off me.

**Brian**   Oh, I see. Sorry Richard.

**Richard**   It's all right.

**Brian**   Shall I come back later?

**Eleanor**   No! Don't leave me alone with him Brian; he's an animal. Besides, it's very stimulating.

**Brian**   What is?

**Eleanor**   Being interrupted.

**Brian** Oh.

**Eleanor** Your popping in and out has given us a lot of pleasure over the years.

**Brian** Oh well, anything to oblige.

**Richard** What do you want, Brian?

**Brian** You haven't heard then?

**Richard** Heard what?

**Brian** I thought I'd be the first. I have the radio on, you see.

**Richard** Heard what?

**Brian** This is going to come as a bit of a shock.

**Richard** What?

**Brian** Rather than tell you over the phone.

**Richard** What?

**Brian** There's no easy way to say this.

**Richard** Just say it.

**Brian** Benny's dead.

**Richard** What?

**Brian** He's dead. They found him this afternoon.

**Richard** Jesus.

*Sits.*

**Richard** Benny.

**Brian** Benny.

**Eleanor** Benny?

**Brian** Yep.

**Eleanor** Benny who?

**Brian**   Benny who!

**Richard**   Benny who?!

**Brian**   Benny Hill.

**Eleanor**   Oh, thank God for that. I thought it was someone we knew.

**Brian**   Being Chairman I thought you'd better know A.S.A.P.

**Richard**   Thanks Bri. I don't believe it.

**Brian**   Nor do I.

**Richard**   Benny Hill.

**Brian**   It's hard to believe. He was found at home.

**Richard**   Heart?

**Brian**   Yep.

**Richard**   Hmm.

**Brian**   That's what I was thinking. Eric, Tommy, Sid. What is it about a comedian's heart?

**Richard**   It's the stress, Brian. A stressed heart just wears out sooner. God likes a good laugh.

**Brian**   So he summons the best, I know. God, life's cruel.

**Eleanor**   Well, thanks for popping over, Brian.

**Brian**   I couldn't have phoned.

**Eleanor**   Got anyone else to tell?

**Brian**   Well, the entire membership should be contacted, really.

**Eleanor**   Well, don't feel you have to stay to comfort us in our grief. You spread the news, we'll comfort each other.

**Brian**   I thought it would be best from the Chairman, really.

**Richard**   You're right. I'll phone round.

**Brian**   I was in the chair when Sid went. I had the honour. Members wept.

**Eleanor**   Sid?

*Pause.*

**All**   James.

**Eleanor**   . . . sorry.

**Richard**   I'll get on with it.

**Eleanor**   Richard.

**Richard**   Would you like a drink?

**Brian**   I suppose a drink would be appropriate, yes.

**Richard**   You know what I'm thinking?

**Brian**   I think I probably do.

**Richard**   Why oh why . . .

**Brian**   I know.

**Richard**   Why would he not appear live?

**Brian**   That's . . .

**Richard**   Eh?

**Brian**   Exactly. Everyone agreed. Benny should have appeared live.

**Eleanor**   He'll have a bit of a job from now on, won't he?

**Richard**   Ellie.

**Eleanor**   What?

**Brian**   You don't understand, Ellie. You see, the man was music hall.

**Richard**   He was.

**Brian**   You can draw a line . . .

**Richard**   A direct line from the greats. From Max Miller . . .

**Brian**   Further.

**Richard**   Further.

**Brian**   From Little Tich . . .

**Richard**   From Dan Leno.

**Brian**   Dan Leno!

**Richard**   You can draw a straight line from Dan Leno through Little Tich, Max Miller, Jimmy James . . . all the way to Benny.

**Brian**   But he wouldn't do live.

**Richard**   He wouldn't.

**Brian**   And that is a tragedy.

**Richard**   And. It's one more nail . . .

**Brian**   I know.

**Richard**   . . . in the coffin of music hall.

**Brian**   That is . . .

**Richard**   Mm?

**Brian**   Absolutely. True.

**Eleanor**   Well Brian, I can tell that at a time like this you'd probably prefer to be alone . . .

**Richard**   Here you go.

**Brian**   What's this then?

**Richard**   It's a martini.

**Brian**   Oh.

**Richard**   To Benny.

**Brian**   To Benny.

**Richard**   I'm not going to make a speech.

**Eleanor** *hides her head.*

**Richard**   Just suffice it to say . . . thanks for making us laugh.

**Brian**   Benny.

**Richard**   Benny.

**Eleanor**   I thought you were the *Dead* Funny Society.

**Richard**   Yes?

**Eleanor**   Well shouldn't you be celebrating then? Lord knows the rest of the country probably is.

**Richard**   Eleanor! Sorry, Brian.

**Eleanor**   It Was A Joke. Of course, neither of you would recognize a joke that didn't have its trousers round its ankles.

**Richard**   Don't talk comedy to us.

**Eleanor**   I wouldn't try to get a word in edgeways.

**Richard**   You have . . . she has absolutely no sense of humour.

**Eleanor**   If I had no sense of humour I would have hung myself from the bannisters on our third wedding anniversary, which in case you've forgotten, we celebrated with a trip to Little and Large. Believe me, I have a sense of humour. I do.

**Brian**   I'd better be off then.

**Richard**   Right. I'll ring round.

**Brian**   And we'll give him a bit of a send-off one night next week, shall we?

**Richard**   Good idea.

**Brian**   Wednesday?

**Richard**   Well, why not?

**Eleanor**   Wednesday?

**Brian**   No one does much on a Wednesday.

**Eleanor**   Lord knows we don't.

**Brian**   Wednesday then. Anyway, sorry to disturb you. I'll
let you get on, nudge nudge say no more. Then again,
you're probably not in the mood any more. I'll see myself
out.

**Eleanor**   Don't slam the door; there's a baby upstairs.

**Brian**   That was quick.

**Richard**   Nick and Lisa's.

**Eleanor**   Just put it on the latch and pull it to.

**Brian**   Will do. Well sir, this is Fred Scuttle saying 'I'll be
seeing you, sir.'

*Laugh. Silence.*

**Brian**   Sad day.

**Eleanor**   I think that just about says it, Brian.

**Richard**   Bye Brian.

**Brian**   Bye.

*Exit* **Brian**.

**Eleanor**   How did his mother know?

**Richard**   What?

**Eleanor**   He was just a tiny baby when she named him
Brian; how could she possibly have known?

**Richard**   There was no need to be rude. These guys
care.

**Eleanor**   So do you.

**Richard**   Yes, so do I.

**Eleanor**   That's what worries me.

**Richard**   What unites us is a very simple thing. The joy of laughter. Alien to you, of course. Risible as far as you're concerned. What are you doing?

**Eleanor**   Putting the clock back.

**Richard**   Ellie.

**Eleanor**   What?

**Richard**   Benny Hill died today.

**Eleanor**   But Richard life, however impoverished, must go on.

**Richard**   You're obsessed.

**Eleanor**   You're sitting there mourning Benny Hill and I'm obsessed? He's probably watching you now. Sitting on a cloud with a television remote in one hand and his penis in the other. Come on Richard, he's saying. Give her one for me.

**Richard**   I've got a lot of phone calls to make.

**Eleanor**   Now?

**Richard**   Yes, now.

*He phones.*

**Richard**   Hello, Toby? Richard. Bit of bad news, mate. Benny Hill passed away. Yes. I know you were. Yes.

**Eleanor** *puts on a video. Pseudo-sensual background music.*

**Richard**   Look, there's a bit of a do at my place next Wednesday. Eight o'clock. Yes. Hard for it to sink in straight away, isn't it? Yes. Yes, absolutely. I must um . . . phone round the others. Bye then.

**Miriam** (*video, simultaneously*)   Hello, my name's Miriam Fairchild. I've been helping loving couples improve their intimate lives for over twenty years, and I hope this video will help you improve yours. We're going to share some of the tenderest moments of sexual expression with three loving couples.

**Richard**   What is she doing on my television set?

**Eleanor**   It's the one she mentioned. I got it in Smiths.

**Miriam** (*video*)   Remember our couples are not actors but genuine loving couples who have volunteered to share with us what they would normally only share between themselves.

**Richard**   Oh, for God's sake. Hello Tracey, is Dave there?

**Miriam** (*video*)   We're going to watch as they explore each other's bodies and as they experiment to bring to each other those gifts of sensual experience that only sex between a loving couple can offer.

**Richard**   Turn it off, will you. Dave? Bit of bad news, mate. (*Beat.*) Oh, you've heard. Right. Yes. Yes. Well, a bit of a do at my place next Wednesday. Eight o'clock. Yeh. Yeh. Yeh.

**Cockney Woman** (*video, simultaneous*)   When Phil first touched my vagina he didn't really know his way about, but since then I've used my own fingers and his to help him learn about all its different parts and what gives me most pleasure.

**Richard**   Bloody hell. Sorry, not you, I was um ... I'll see you and your wife next week then Phil. I mean Dave. And Tracey, yes. Cheers then, bye.

**Cockney Man** (*video*)   What I've found out is most important is to be gentle and understanding, not go at it like a bull in a china shop sort of thing. And to keep a steady rhythm.

**Cockney Woman** (*video*)   What I really love is for Phil to use his tongue. I think at first we were both afraid of oral sex, but now it's quite a favourite. In fact sometimes that's all we do for an entire evening.

**Eleanor**   Jesus.

**Richard**   Bloody hell.

**Eleanor**   Is she really doing that?

**Richard**   Well where's it gone if she isn't?

**Miriam** (*video*)   Above all, it's important for a couple to talk to each other.

**Eleanor**   Unless they've got their mouths full of course.

**Miriam** (*video*)   Don't be afraid to tell your partner exactly what pleases you most.

**Cockney Man** (*video*)   Foreplay's a movable feast really. Sometimes it lasts a long time and sometimes we both get aroused really quickly.

**Eleanor**   They're going to, aren't they?

**Cockney Woman** (*video*)   Making love to Phil has become, over time, the most exciting thing in my life.

**Richard**   I've read about this couple.

**Cockney Woman** (*video*)   It's brought us closer, and helped us to a greater understanding of one another as human beings.

**Richard**   They met at the audition, apparently.

**Eleanor**   Don't be ridiculous.

**Richard**   It's true.

**Eleanor**   He hasn't got a condom on.

*They watch. Enter* **Nick**, *quietly, intending to surprise them. Freezes.*

**Cockney Woman** (*video*)   Whenever I find myself approaching orgasm now I feel free to really let myself go.

And so does Phil.

*Sound of approaching climaxes.* **Nick** *very quietly tries to creep backwards out of the room.* **Lisa** *enters behind him.*

**Lisa**    Only us.

**Richard** *and* **Eleanor** *leap up, fumble for the remote, and turn off the TV.*

**Nick**    Hi.

**Eleanor**    Hello, Nick.

**Richard**    Hi.

**Lisa**    Hi. Is he all right?

**Eleanor**    Who?

**Lisa**    The baby.

**Richard**    Baby?

**Eleanor**    What baby?

**Lisa**    My baby.

**Eleanor**    Oh, he's fine. Fast asleep.

**Nick**    Sorry if we er . . .

**Lisa**    I said you'd scare the daylights out of them. Lord knows what you might have been doing, privacy of your own home.

**Nick**    The door was on the latch.

**Eleanor**    We were just . . . watching TV.

**Nick**    Were you?

**Richard**    Yes, just um . . .

**Eleanor**    A programme.

**Richard**    A video.

**Eleanor**    A video.

**Richard**  A programme.

**Nick**  I'd only just come in, I was um . . .

**Richard**  Some rubbish, anyway.

**Nick**  Right. Wednesdays.

**Lisa**  What were you watching?

**Nick**  I love this rug. Lisa? Haven't you always loved this rug?

**Lisa**  Umm.

**Nick**  Great rug.

**Lisa**  It's a lovely rug, yes.

**Nick**  And so much nicer on the wall than it would be on the floor.

**Richard**  Well, we like it there, anyway.

**Eleanor**  At least you can't trip over it.

**Lisa**  I like a nice video. What did you get out?

**Richard**  There's always a flaw, of course. There's always a deliberate flaw woven into the design so as not to offend the perfection of Allah.

**Nick**  Really?

**Lisa**  Comedy or horror?

**Eleanor**  Of course in this one there's a number of flaws.

**Nick**  What does that signify?

**Eleanor**  A cheap carpet.

*They laugh.* **Lisa** *moves away from the rug.*

**Lisa**  Nice evening indoors, a glass of wine and a good video.

**Nick**  There's the flaw. Look.

**Lisa**   Lovely.

**Nick**   Look.

**Lisa**   I've looked.

**Nick**   No, but look.

**Lisa**   They've got a lot of lovely things, Nick. I've always said Ellie; the way you've decorated this house makes me wish I had the same taste.

*She picks up the cassette box, looks at it, turns it upside down, drops it.*

**Lisa**   And you're right about the rug; it's beautiful. Oh look, there's a little cat.

**Eleanor**   Camel.

**Lisa**   Camel.

**Richard**   Anyway.

**Lisa**   Anyway.

**Nick**   Right.

**Richard**   Drinks!

**Nick**   Lovely.

**Lisa**   Sorry if we're a bit early.

**Nick**   Didn't stay for the second half.

**Richard**   What did you go and see?

**Nick**   Starlight Express.

**Richard**   Not very good?

**Nick**   Oh no, excellent. Excellent. Gave Lisa a headache.

**Lisa**   It wasn't the show, Nick. When I get a headache it's for a reason.

**Richard**   Right.

**Lisa**    I immediately think; something's wrong.

**Nick**    She immediately thought; Ellie's dropped the baby down the stairs.

**Lisa**    No I didn't.

**Nick**    That's what you said.

**Lisa**    No I didn't.

**Nick**    Ellie's fed the baby bleach instead of apple juice and buried it in the garden.

**Lisa**    Nick. Ellie, I trust you completely, or I wouldn't have left him in the first place. You're really getting on my nerves lately. Where is he?

**Eleanor**    Under the lawn just beside the cherry tree. It's a lovely spot.

**Lisa**    When you become a mother Ellie, you'll realize; certain things aren't funny any more.

**Nick**    Husbands. Life.

**Eleanor**    He's fine. He's upstairs. Do you need a paracetamol?

**Lisa**    Oh no, I just have to wait 'til it passes.

**Richard**    You won't have heard the news then.

**Nick**    What?

**Richard**    Benny Hill.

**Nick**    What?

**Richard**    Died.

**Nick**    No.

**Richard**    Yep.

**Nick**    Jesus. What a bloody shame.

**Lisa**    I knew it.

**Richard**   What?

**Lisa**   My headache.

**Nick**   Don't be ridiculous.

**Lisa**   Whenever I get a headache like that, somebody somewhere dies.

**Nick**   Statistically speaking of course, a few million more peg it every time you blow your nose.

**Eleanor**   What's wrong with you?

**Lisa**   One of the chorus skated over his cellphone.

**Richard**   Cellphone?

**Nick**   Month's trial.

**Lisa**   I think I'll go and see our son.

**Eleanor**   I'll show you.

**Lisa**   No one ever phones you at home, let alone somewhere else. He's had it a fortnight; it hasn't rung yet.

*Exit* **Lisa** *and* **Eleanor**.

**Nick**   Poor old Benny. He'll have left a few bob.

**Richard**   I should think so.

**Nick**   Mean old bugger apparently. Worse than Doddy.

**Richard**   Fear. That's what it is.

**Nick**   Fear?

**Richard**   That the crowd'll turn, the laughter stop. Fear of penury.

**Nick**   Look at Frankie.

**Richard**   Perfect example.

**Nick**   Out of work 1957 to 1963, then again all through the eighties. And that's a man with staggering talent.

**Richard**   Must be frightening.

**Nick**   I should say so. Yes missus.

**Both**   I've never been so insulted.

**Nick**   Oh . . . please yourselves! Bit sexist of course, Benny Hill.

**Richard**   Not in an offensive way, though.

**Nick**   No, no. I meant in a women-with-big-tits-and-short-skirts-bending-over-a-lot sort of way.

**Richard**   Absolutely.

**Nick**   Nice work if you can get it. I'll bet he died with a smile on his face.

**Richard**   How is work?

**Nick**   I can't stand it. And I'm earning a pittance. I should have studied harder you know, when we were young. You shouldn't have encouraged me to be such a nerd. I mean if you got through med. school, anyone could have.

**Richard**   You put on some good revues.

**Nick**   I should have studied. I've got the brain you know.

**Richard**   It wasn't your brain got you thrown out; it was the May ball.

**Nick**   It was class prejudice.

**Richard**   It was the penis sewn to the inside of your trouser leg.

**Nick**   I was going to put it back. It's not as if one borrowed dick was going to halt the advance of medical science. I could have been a surgeon.

**Richard**   Oh, you showed great promise.

**Nick**   I mean admit it; it's not that difficult. Takes more bottle than skill. A car mechanic knows more than a surgeon; he knows his way around a Ford, a Vauxhall, a Toyota. But bodies; been inside one, been inside them all. Find the bit that's not working and whip it out. I could do that. There's nothing I don't know about a Vauxhall Astra.

**Richard**  You're better off out of it.

**Nick**  Or the Cavalier.

**Richard**  It gets you down in the end.

**Nick**  Falling apart, of course.

**Richard**  What?

**Nick**  The Astra.

**Richard**  Oh.

**Nick**  And I'm thirty-six!

**Richard**  Don't you start.

**Nick**  They've put me in change of the sixth-form. Two boys, eleven girls. I'm not joking Richard, these girls. I mean it's nine-thirty on a Tuesday morning and I've got to get from registration to the biology block with a hard-on the size of a chalk duster. Which is tricky when you're teaching a class of seventeen-year-olds what to do with one. And this National Curriculum's a bit bloody specific. I used to whap on the old Shell video and leave the rest to filter down from the back row. Now we have to discuss it within a moral frame of reference. I'd rather discuss it in the back of the Astra. With Halford, Jenny.

**Richard**  You wouldn't, would you?

**Nick**  I did once.

**Richard**  Really?

**Nick**  Never again. Trouble with seventeen-year-olds; they're so bloody immature. And prudish when you get down to it.

**Richard**  Bit of a risk, wasn't it?

**Nick**   Came a bit close. Luckily she needed 2 B's and a C to do Chemistry at Hull. Promised not to wreck my career if I fiddled her multiple choice. Never again. It's not just the money I envy you; it's all those nurses I regret. Nurses know what's what.

**Richard**   I wouldn't know.

*Cellphone rings.* **Nick** *answers eagerly.*

**Nick**   Excuse me. Hello? Hello? Ah.

**Richard**   What?

**Nick**   Battery. Tells you when it needs re-charging.

**Richard**   Really?

**Nick**   Oh yes. It's very user-friendly.

**Richard** *takes the phone.* **Eleanor** *and* **Lisa** *return, the latter with carry cot.*

**Lisa**   Here he is then. Fast asleep.

**Nick**   Fully networked; take it anywhere.

**Richard**   Uhuh.

**Lisa**   Thanks, Ellie.

**Eleanor**   That's all right. Any time.

**Nick**   Twelve number memory, call back; the lot.

**Richard**   Nice and light.

**Nick**   Oh, yes.

**Lisa**   Oh, look.

**Eleanor**   He's lovely.

**Lisa**   He is, isn't he? Nick, look.

**Nick**   Yeh.

**Lisa**   Look, Richard.

**Richard**   Right.

**Lisa**   Have a look. Sweet. He's so sweet. You've got your mummy's mouth, haven't you?

**Nick**   Certainly has.

**Lisa**   But you've got your Daddy's eyes. He's got your eyes, Nick.

**Nick**   He's got your father's nose. (*Laughs.*) Hya hya hya.

**Richard**   What?

**Lisa**   Nick.

**Nick**   Thirty-two quid a month, plus airtime.

**Lisa**   It's hard sometimes, for fathers to bond. They haven't been through the pain, you see. They haven't got the chemicals. When you give birth Ellie, when you give life ... it's ... well, you feel connected to something that well, goes on beyond your own ... I don't know ... your past, or your future. You become more ... what's the word? Mortal, or the other thing; I can never remember the word. Anyway; you know you'll never be the same again. It's so ... it's really, it's ...

**Nick**   Can I use those jump leads?

**Richard**   Sure. They're in my boot.

**Lisa**   We'd better get him home.

**Richard**   I'll give you a hand.

**Nick**   Thanks, mate.

**Lisa**   I'll bring him out when it's going.

*The men leave.*

I didn't say what he said I said. About you dropping the baby, not down the stairs.

**Eleanor**   I'm sure you didn't.

**Lisa**   It's strange though, when you're a little bit psychic. You know when something happens, but not always exactly what. Until later.

**Eleanor**   I see.

**Lisa**   (*mouths*)   How are things?

**Eleanor**   What?

**Lisa**   (*mouths*)   How are things?

**Eleanor**   Things are fine, except I seem to have just gone deaf. What things?

**Lisa**   Things, you know.

**Eleanor**   Worse if anything.

**Lisa**   Nick's got very strange since the baby.

**Eleanor**   Oh, we'll sort something out.

**Lisa**   You need a common interest, that's what you need. That's what Nick and I have. Not just the society; we've cultivated many common interests. We've got dozens of common interests. Well at least I have. Nick's a bit moody at the moment; he's not got much interest in anything. Why don't you come to an appreciation evening? It really is great fun. When we put up Hattie's plaque in Ickenham it was really moving. And Mrs Gardner, she's not a member but she's the lady who lives in the house where Hattie was born and she was very supportive, she invited us all in and she'd been to the video shop and got out *Carry On Matron* and we all sat and watched and Ellie, we laughed. And Richard was wearing the matron's cap; you know, the one that Hattie wore that my mum had in her cabinet; oh, he looked a sight, but anyway he turned to me and he said 'You know Lisa, I wish Ellie was here.'

**Eleanor**   Did he?

**Lisa**   Mmmm.

**Eleanor**   No he didn't. God, you're a terrible liar.

**Lisa**   Well, he had a look on his face as much as to say.

**Eleanor**   I've tried joining in; you know that. It's hopeless. I don't find anything funny any more.

**Lisa**   Well Ellie, humour's a funny thing.

**Eleanor**   Not in my experience.

**Lisa**   Men will laugh at anything.

**Eleanor**   Except themselves.

**Lisa**   I speak of course as the only female member.

**Eleanor**   I don't know how you can bear them all en masse.

**Lisa**   Oh I know; all those men, and only one female member. I wonder what I think I'm doing there sometimes. I suppose it's just ... well, you know; when you've been in the business.

**Eleanor**   You only danced for three summer seasons.

**Lisa**   I did sketches too.

**Eleanor**   In Bournemouth.

**Lisa**   Library sketch. Hospital sketch.

**Eleanor**   Big breaths, nurse.

**Lisa**   Yeth, and I'm only theventeen. Of course my mum was in show business all her life. All those Carry Ons. I pointed her out in *Carry On Matron*; she's in the bed by the door whenever they walk past. The men loved that you see. That's why I like to turn up. I'm a sort of link for them; to the real thing.

**Eleanor**   You're the least they deserve.

**Richard** *enters.*

**Richard**   Well, it's going. I'd get in quick if I were you.

**Lisa**   Ooh, right. Listen Ellie, thanks again.

**Eleanor**    Any time.

**Lisa**    And thank you Richard.

**Richard**    That's all right.

**Lisa**    Bye then.

**Richard**    Bye.

**Eleanor** *shows her out.*

**Lisa**    And remember what I said.

**Eleanor**    I will. Bye.

**Lisa**    Bye.

**Eleanor** *returns.*

**Richard**    What did she say?

**Eleanor**    If what Lisa said went in one ear and out the other it would be a blessing. Unfortunately it goes in one ear, and bounces round the cranium for hours.

**Richard**    What were you talking about?

**Eleanor**    Not you.

**Richard**    Good. I think I'll turn in.

**Eleanor**    Well, it is way past your bedtime. I bought this Mills and Boon today for fifty pee. Look. That's you and me on the front, the day we met. You had a stethoscope sticking out of your pocket and I was a shy young thing. Well, it's almost us. She hasn't got her feet in stirrups, of course.

**Richard**    Eleanor.

**Eleanor**    There I was, untangling my knickers from my tights, and Dr Kildare asks me out to dinner. Was it love at first sight?

**Richard**    No, it was serious professional misconduct.

**Eleanor**    Three words it turns out you don't know the

meaning of.

**Richard**  I wish you'd listen to yourself sometimes.

**Eleanor**  I do. I know. I sound like that poor old cow in all those second-rate sitcoms. The one who's desperate to sleep with Reg Varney. Or Sid or Benny or some other fat ugly bastard. Only one joke and it's always on her, because they're not interested. They don't want her. They want the pneumatic bimbo who lives next door.

**Richard**  There's no one else.

**Eleanor**  It's just me then?

**Richard**  It's not you. It's me. It's what I do, it's who I am, it's . . . I don't know.

**Eleanor**  It's not necessarily your fault.

**Richard**  It is my fault. But it's not my problem. I can only feel what I feel.

**Eleanor**  Nothing for me or nothing at all?

**Richard**  Nothing much.

**Eleanor**  You pursued me with such ardour, such passion. I fought it so hard, loving you. But I did, and I do. And it's indescribably painful trying not to.

*He goes to bed. The lights fade.*


**Scene Two**

*The same. One week later.* **Richard** *alone.*

**Richard**  The comic traditions of this small island are the envy of the world. France has its rural whimsy. America its Jewish wit. Belgium its Belgians. No, but seriously. One nation stands out when it comes to comedy. Ask a Norwegian, a Canadian, a native Australian, they'll all tell you; the English are funny.

**Eleanor** *appears listening.*

**Richard**  And the undisputed King of British comedy was of course, indeed still is . . . Benny Hill. But it's not only those Joe Soaps, those Mr and Mrs Averages who number themselves among his fans. Mention should also be made of Greta Garbo. Michael Jackson. The Queen Mother.

**Eleanor**  The Ayatollah Khomeni. Saddam Hussein.

**Richard**  I didn't know you were in.

**Eleanor**  I fell asleep.

**Richard**  Have you been drinking?

**Eleanor**  I only drink at mealtimes.

**Richard**  What did you have for lunch?

**Eleanor**  Three martinis and an orgasm.

**Richard**  Are you going out?

**Eleanor**  Tonight's the night is it? Farewell Fred Scuttle?

**Richard**  Yes.

**Eleanor**  I wouldn't miss it for the world. I've got a class at seven, but I'll be back!

**Richard**  You're drinking too much.

**Eleanor**  I'm drinking just enough. For a Wednesday.

**Richard**  Don't start.

**Eleanor**  When are the anoraks arriving?

**Richard**  They don't all wear anoraks.

**Eleanor**  They do.

**Richard**  That is a generalization.

**Eleanor**  Every one of them wears an anorak.

**Richard**  Inaccurate stereotyping.

**Eleanor**   I know they don't call them anoraks any more, but if it's day-glo and padded and makes you look like a cuddly hand grenade then as far as I'm concerned it's an anorak.

**Richard**   I'm willing to admit not all of them have an IQ of a hundred and fifty . . .

**Eleanor**   Put together.

**Richard**   . . . and it's very easy to take the mickey out of a group of people bonded by a common interest . . .

**Eleanor**   Sorry.

**Richard**   . . . but there's no need for this unending stream of abuse.

**Eleanor**   I'm sorry. I've got a surprise for you later.

**Richard**   What?

*Doorbell.*

**Eleanor**   Hello Brian.

**Richard** *goes to the door.* **Eleanor** *drinks.*

**Richard**   Hello, Brian.

**Brian** *enters with shopping.*

**Brian**   I'm very upset. I've just had a dreadful row and you know me; I don't have arguments, but he's really upset me.

**Richard**   Who?

**Brian**   Who do you think? Les Rollins.

**Richard**   Ah.

**Brian**   Anyway, I've been to Tescos and I've baked a cake. Hello Ellie.

**Eleanor**   Hello Brian.

**Brian**   What's this?

**Eleanor**   A key to the door; you'll be in and out all evening.

**Brian**   Ooh, only if my luck changes. Ta. Anyway, Rollins phoned me about tonight and says, what's all this he hears about fancy dress? I said it's not fancy dress, it's a token gesture. Token gesture my arse, he says. I'm not coming dressed up! I tried to explain it's a little tradition the society likes to uphold and that it wasn't fancy dress, it was just a visual tribute and you didn't have to go the whole hog. Just a beret or some rimless specs or slicked back hair and Chinese glasses, whatever . . . a *tribute*.

**Richard**   That's right.

**Brian**   Well, he wouldn't have it. Said it was farcical. I was a bit rude, I said, if you don't like it, don't come.

**Eleanor**   Maybe he's got a point.

**Brian**   What?

**Eleanor**   Well. It's a bit undignified, isn't it?

**Brian**   There is nothing undignified about humbling oneself and donning the symbolic garb of a great clown.

**Richard**   Of course not.

**Eleanor**   It's just that some people look a bit funny dressed up in a bald wig and baggy trousers; not you Brian, but some people.

**Brian**   You think he's right? You think we should just abandon one of our silliest traditions just because Les Rollins 'feels a bit peculiar'?! He likes Ben Elton, you know. Les Rollins is a big fan of Ben Elton. What does that tell you?

**Richard**   Don't get upset, Brian.

**Brian**   I am upset. I'm very upset. Ever since he joined there's been contention in the air. I knew he was going to be trouble when he turned up to his first meeting with that video of Tommy Cooper's last performance, and his fatal collapse. I was appalled.

**Richard**   There was quite a healthy majority wanted to see it, Brian.

**Eleanor**   Seventeen to one, wasn't it?

**Brian**   I was ashamed of you. I thought you at least had good taste. That upset me, that show of hands. I couldn't watch.

**Richard**   You should have. It was actually very dignified.

**Eleanor**   A man holding a rubber chicken having a coronary in front of fifteen hundred people? Dignified?

**Brian**   Exactly.

**Richard**   He was plying his craft, he paused, and then he fell like an oak. Yes. Dignified.

**Eleanor**   First trick he ever got right, I know that.

**Brian**   It wasn't even a first generation tape; it was a grainy old bootleg.

**Richard**   Bit of history though.

**Brian**   It was a snuff movie. I knew we'd rue the day we voted Les Rollins in. I'm not at all sure any more about a lot of the membership, to tell you the truth. I've seen the *Bottom* videos surreptitiously passed during coffee break. There doesn't seem to be any discrimination any more between good old bawdy innuendo and filth. Between good old slapstick and sick physical violence. Maybe I'm getting old. He hasn't said anyting to you has he? Rollins?

**Richard**   What about?

**Brian**   Me?

**Richard**   No.

**Brian**   Anyway, that's the bad news.

**Eleanor**   There's good news is there?

**Brian**   There's very good news. We've got a guest of honour. Don't ask me how I got his phone number, but I did. And you know my philosophy; if you don't ask you don't get. So I phoned and I asked and he said he'd be honoured.

**Richard**   Who?

**Brian**   Honoured. I nearly fell off my chair.

**Richard**   Who?

**Brian**   Henry McGee.

**Richard**   No.

**Brian**   Yes.

**Richard**   Henry McGee?

**Brian**   Yes.

**Richard**   I don't believe you.

**Brian**   Henry McGee.

**Eleanor**   In my house?

**Brian**   He was totally charming. He said of course he'd heard of us. He'd seen us on the news doing Hattie's plaque. And he said he'd be honoured to join with us in remembering Benny.

**Richard**   That's extraordinary.

**Brian**   Then he went a bit quiet. You know.

**Richard**   Right.

**Brian**   Then he said . . . I miss him, of course.

**Richard**   Did he?

**Brian**   'I miss him, of course.' Then he asked if I'd like to see *It Runs in the Family*. He's currently appearing in *It Runs in the Family*.

**Eleanor**   Benny Hill?

**Brian**   Henry McGee.

**Eleanor**   Oh. I was going to say. In fact, I was going to go.

**Brian**   He said I should definitely see it, Ray Cooney being a master of the genre. And let him know I was coming.

**Richard**   He offered you tickets?

**Brian**   No, just to let him know when I'd got tickets, I suppose to see him afterwards.

**Richard**   That's . . .

**Brian**   He was very charming on the phone.

**Richard**   I'm not surprised though.

**Brian**   A charming man. 'I miss him, of course.'

**Eleanor**   Well, that's a bit of a coup isn't it, Brian?

**Brian**   I know.

**Eleanor**   Step up from Bella Emberg.

**Brian**   Oh, now, now. Bella was . . .

**Richard**   Ellie.

**Eleanor**   Oh, she was.

**Brian**   She was very kind to fit us in to what was for her a pretty hectic Madhouse season.

**Eleanor**   I know. I know. She was very kind. And startlingly articulate. I think Bella Emberg was almost as articulate as she was thin.

**Brian**   Can I unpack this lot in the kitchen?

**Richard**   Of course.

*Exit* **Brian**.

**Eleanor**  I shouldn't have said that.

**Richard**  You're getting very cruel.

**Eleanor**  I know.

**Richard**  I mean; poor Brian.

**Eleanor**  I mean poor Bella. She was sweet.

**Brian** (*off*)  I've catered for twenty.

**Eleanor**  Twenty?

**Brian**  But if they all turn up there should be enough.

**Eleanor**  You said half a dozen.

**Brian** (*off*)  Oh, and I had a bit of a stroke in Tescos.

**Eleanor**  I bet that had them rolling in the aisles. Where can I get the video?

**Brian**  Look. Custard pies.

**Eleanor**  What for?

**Brian**  Just a joke. I shouldn't think anyone'll actually throw one.

**Eleanor**  I should bloody well hope not.

**Brian**  Do you think it's living dangerously? Because I needn't put them out.

**Richard**  No, it's a nice idea.

**Eleanor**  So was the Titanic.

**Brian**  Can I help myself to plates?

**Richard**  Yes.

*Exit* **Brian**.

**Richard**  This means a lot to Brian.

**Eleanor**  So?

**Richard**  Why are you trying to spoil it for him?

**Eleanor**   Time of the month.

**Richard**   Couldn't we call a truce, just for tonight?

*Pause.*

**Eleanor**   I suppose a fuck's out of the question?

**Richard**   If you're that desperate, have an affair.

*Enter* **Brian**.

**Brian**   It's very good of you both. I gave serious thought to using my flat now that Mum's not there. But it's so small. I thought if I opened it out and used Mum's room, but that'd feel very strange because I'm not using Mum's room yet. I'm still in the small back room, but I have laid out the dining area in the living room as my office area now. I use the big table and to eat I use the television table I got Mum from Argos. All in all it's nice to have the extra space; I know she wouldn't mind me saying that; she used to say much the same herself. But her room's much as she left it. Which reminds me Ellie, I keep forgetting to bring you that perfume . . .

**Eleanor**   Oh, that's all right.

**Brian**   No no, I've remembered.

*Gives her a bottle of stale 4711 and a minuscule bottle of Chanel no 4.*

**Brian**   She'd have liked you to have it. She liked you.

**Eleanor**   Thank you.

**Brian**   I've got some sausage rolls. Can I pop them in the oven?

**Eleanor**   You can pop anything in my oven any time you like, Brian.

**Brian**   Oh well, if you weren't spoken for.

**Eleanor**   I'm not even spoken *to*. Richard wouldn't mind.

**Brian**   Oh well then, I'll whisk you away.

**Eleanor**   Yes please. Thanks for this.

**Brian** *exits.*

**Eleanor**   Who with?

**Richard**   What?

**Eleanor**   An affair?

**Richard**   Well, that would be your choice, wouldn't it?

**Eleanor**   Oh, thanks. All right. I'll have an affair with Nick.

**Richard**   Nick? You always said he had a face like a turtle.

**Eleanor**   You don't have to look at the mantelpiece Richard, when you're sitting on it.

**Brian** *enters.*

**Brian**   Right, that's me done for now. I'm just going to nip home and put my frock on. Nick is bringing the wine now, isn't he?

**Richard**   I hope so.

**Brian**   I'll see you later then. What a performance.

**Brian** *leaves.*

**Richard**   What I meant was you don't have to lead a celibate life just because I choose to. You are allowed to choose.

**Eleanor**   I chose you. We're supposed to have chosen each other. We're supposed to be a couple. Couples make love.

**Richard**   Not the couples I know.

**Eleanor**   Yes they do.

**Richard**   They don't you know.

**Eleanor**   Well the couples I know do. It's normal.

**Richard**   It doesn't feel normal.

**Eleanor**   It's perfectly normal for most people.

**Richard**   I'm not most people.

**Eleanor**   Exactly; you're not normal.

**Richard**   I'm perfectly normal.

**Eleanor**   If you were normal, we'd have a sex life!

**Richard**   I can't stand these conversations going round and round . . .

**Eleanor**   We have to discuss things; it's part of the process.

**Richard**   Part of the pressure.

**Eleanor**   There is no pressure.

**Richard**   Pressure from Miriam, pressure from you.

**Eleanor**   I don't want to pressure you.

**Richard**   Don't then.

**Eleanor**   But I can't ignore this . . . misery I feel.

**Richard**   This is my body. It's not yours. It's mine. It doesn't want to be touched. That doesn't make me particularly happy, but it feels perfectly normal.

*Doorbell.*

**Eleanor**   I'm going to rip that doorbell out with my teeth. I gave you the key, Brian!

*She goes to the door.* **Nick** *and* **Lisa** *enter, with carry cot.*

**Eleanor** (*off*)   Oh. Hello.

**Lisa**   I know we're early, I know. I told him we were going to be early.

**Nick**   Sorry.

**Eleanor**   That's all right; the party's started.

**Richard**   Hi, Nick.

**Nick**   Hi.

**Lisa**   Can I take him straight upstairs?

**Eleanor**   Sure.

**Lisa** *exits.*

**Nick**   Sorry we're early. Bit of a snag. I couldn't get any cash out of the machine for the booze.

**Richard**   Been embezzling the funds, have you?

**Nick**   No, no. I don't know; it just ate the card. Thing is, we're a bit short ourselves at the moment.

**Richard**   I'll give you some.

**Nick**   Cheers mate. There's a second card you see, that Brian used to have, but he swears he gave it back to me. Oh, it'll sort itself out. Ta, mate. I'd better rush; I've left the car running.

**Eleanor**   If you're going to Threshers, you can give me a lift to the Poly.

**Nick**   Sure.

**Eleanor**   I'll give you a blow job on the way.

**Nick**   Splendid. She's a wonderful woman, your wife. Nothing's too much trouble, is it?

**Richard**   See you later.

**Nick**   Right. Come on then; let's hope we don't hit any potholes.

*Exit* **Nick**.

**Eleanor**   It'd give him a hell of a shock if I did, wouldn't it?

**Richard**   Go to work, Ellie.

*Exit* **Ellie** *as* **Lisa** *comes downstairs.*

**Eleanor** (*off*)   Bye, Lisa!

**Lisa** (*off*)   Oh. Bye. She go with him?

**Richard**   She's got a class.

**Lisa**   Oh, I see.

*She takes off her coat; dressed in a severe woollen twin-set and pearls.*

**Lisa**   Da da! Nick wanted me to come as a Hill's Angel of course, but I told him he'd got another think coming. So I've come as a spinster. Well, it was either bimbo, battle axe or spinster and I'm certainly not a battle axe, am I?

*She poses.* **Richard** *sips his drink. She sits.*

Norman Wisdom was very good, wasn't he? I'd have enjoyed it more if I hadn't been stuck on the end next to Les Rollins. He kept saying whatever it was Norman was going to say just before he said it, and he's a very tactile person, isn't he, Les? Very wide to sit next to. Squeezes past when there's bags of room. Holds his glass at nipple height so he can brush you with his knuckles. He's been paying me quite a lot of attention actually; I've been wondering if I should mention it to Nick.

**Richard** *goes to her. She stands. He lifts his hand to fondle her breast. She moves away.*

**Lisa**   I've had this headache threatening me all day. Did you see 'It'll Be Alright on the Night'? Dennis Norden said something very interesting. He said apparently Sigmund Freud said there were only four kinds of joke.

**Richard** *closes the door, gently bends her over the back of the sofa.*

**Lisa**   I taped it actually. Apparently, let's see if I can get this right . . .

**Richard** *pulls down her knickers and unzips his fly.*

**Lisa**   There's . . . Concealment of Knowledge Later

Revealed, Substitution of One Concept for Another.
Um . . . Unexpected Conclusion to a Hitherto Logical
Progression, and um . . .

*He enters her.*

Oh. Something else.

*They fuck.*

Hard.

*Enter* **Benny Hill** *in long mac, beret and pebble glasses.*

**Brian**    Here I am then.

**Lisa** *head first over the sofa,* **Richard** *zips up fly before first
securing penis.*

**Brian**    Only me.

# Act Two

## Scene One

*The same. A moment later.*

**Brian**  Mind you; I can't see a thing through these glasses. Oh, hello, Lisa.

**Lisa**  Hello Brian.

**Brian**  How are you?

**Lisa**  I've got a terrible headache.

**Brian**  Poor thing.

**Lisa**  . Excuse me.

*Exit* **Lisa**, *squinting oddly, walking into door frame.*

**Richard**  She gets these headaches.

**Brian**  Well, some cures are more enjoyable than others, I suppose. Sorry, Richard.

**Richard**  Lisa and I, we're strictly um . . .

**Brian**  Oh, live and let live, me. I may seem old-fashioned, but not a lot surprises me.

**Richard**  Seriously though.

**Brian**  Oh, quite seriously. I was never here.

**Richard**  What time is it?

**Brian**  It's ten past . . . oooh, I must get a little hand put on this watch. Seven. (*Fred Scuttle*) So sir, this is Fred Scuttle reporting for duty sir.

*Enter* **Lisa**.

**Brian**  Oh, here she is then.

**Lisa**   Lo, Brian.

**Brian**   How's your head?

**Lisa**   Not so bad, but I've lost a contact lens. Don't walk about! Have you got a torch?

**Richard**   In the shed I think. I'll um . . .

*Exit* **Richard**.

**Lisa**   Listen Brian, what we were . . . well, just now . . . I don't know what came over me.

**Brian**   Well, Richard presumably.

**Lisa**   Brian!

**Brian**   Sorry.

**Lisa**   Honestly.

**Brian**   Wash your mouth out, Brian. Is that it?

**Lisa**   Oh. Yes. Thank you.

*She puts her lens in.*

**Lisa**   The thing is I don't do things like that. This. What I just did.

**Brian**   Lisa; I'm see no evil, hear no evil, speak utter filth, me. But I'm very discreet.

**Lisa**   The thing is I'm a happily married woman.

**Brian**   I know. And long may you remain so. Mum's the word.

**Lisa**   Thanks Brian.

*Her head hurts.*

**Brian**   I get nervous when you've got a headache. I wonder which of us is going to pop off next.

**Lisa**   Don't joke about it Brian. It's a gift, but it can also be a burden.

**Brian**   Oh, I can imagine.

**Lisa**   And people do tend to make you an object of mockery.

**Brian**   Not me.

**Lisa**   No, not you.

**Brian**   There's something I've been meaning to ask. Have you ever tried to ... well, communicate with the other side?

**Lisa**   Um well, not for entertainment purposes, if that's what you mean.

**Brian**   Oh no; of course not. But have you never been tempted to speak to ... I don't know ... to Hancock maybe. Ask him why he did something as silly as that? Tell him how much we miss him?

**Lisa**   Well, there have been times when ... when I think I've made contact, yes.

**Brian**   Oh.

**Lisa**   Three times, as a matter of fact.

**Brian**   Mmm?

**Lisa**   Once with Hancock, yes.

**Brian**   Oh, sweetheart.

**Lisa**   He came to me. I didn't call him up or anything. He came to me when they gave me my epidural.

**Brian**   How was he?

**Lisa**   Not very happy. I'd been in labour twelve hours. He said I should fight the desire I had at the time to die. Said the afterlife wasn't all it was cracked up to be.

**Brian**   Good Lord.

**Lisa**   Something about long queues. Once, this was years ago, was Eric.

**Brian**   Eric!

**Lisa**   Eric Morecambe came to me. Just after he died. I could tell it was him from a long way off because of the sock suspenders just below the hem of his toga. Now he was very happy.

**Brian**   Oh, I'm glad; he deserves to be.

**Lisa**   He sent a little message for Ern. I dropped him a note.

**Brian**   What did it say?

**Lisa**   Sorry about the early retirement. Don't let them get you on 'Celebrity Squares'.

**Brian**   Joking to the end.

**Lisa**   And beyond really, Brian.

**Brian**   Who else?

**Lisa**   Well, I'm not sure about this one, but Max Miller, I think.

**Brian**   Bless you. What did he say?

**Lisa**   It wasn't so much what he said . . .

**Brian**   It was the way he said it.

**Lisa**   No, it was just his . . . presence. I think it was him.

**Brian**   What was he wearing?

**Lisa**   I didn't actually see him. His voice came out of the wallpaper. Lovely flowery wallpaper.

**Brian**   Oh, that was Maxie.

**Lisa**   I think it was.

**Brian**   There'll never be another.

**Lisa**   Best of all though . . .

**Brian**   Who?

**Lisa**    My dad.

*Enter* **Richard**.

**Lisa**    I've found it, thanks.

**Richard**    Right.

**Brian**    This woman's got a gift, you know. Well, I know you know. I'm sorry, I've got a mind like a litter tray. And I've not started drinking yet. Well, only a small gin at tea time.

**Richard**    Would you like a drink?

**Lisa**    Yes please.

**Brian**    You've twisted my arm.

*Doorbell.* **Brian** *rises.*

**Richard**    It's all right, Brian.

**Richard** *goes.*

**Brian**    So is it possible to actually speak to someone on the other side?

**Lisa**    Brian, I'm not going to call up Benny Hill.

**Brian**    No, no. That's not what I meant.

**Lisa**    I wouldn't want to distract him if he's making his way through limbo or something.

**Brian**    No, I mean if there was someone and there were things you never said.

*Enter* **Nick**, *dressed as Benny Hill's Mr Chow Mein character and carrying a box of booze.*

**Nick** (*cod Japanese*)    Ah, harrow. And a velly good evenin to you.

**Brian**    Ohh! You look fabulous! He looks just like him, doesn't he? You look just like him.

**Nick**    Ahh, an you fried skull. Fried skull.

**Brian**   Oh, Fred Scuttle. That's right. That's me, sir.

**Nick**   Preased to meet you.

**Brian**   Pleased to meet you, sir.

**Lisa**   Can I have that drink?

**Brian**   You've not made much of an effort.

**Richard**   All in good time, Brian.

**Brian**   And there's hardly any food out.

**Richard**   I've been busy.

**Nick**   He slip in his cock?

**Lisa**   What?

**Nick**   He slip in his cock?

**Lisa**   Um . . .

**Brian**   I'll get the dips.

*Exit* **Brian**.

**Nick**   He slip in his cock?

**Richard**   Um . . .

**Nick**   A *baby*!

**Lisa**   What?

**Nick**   Is *the baby* asleep in his cot?

**Lisa**   Oh!

**Richard**   Oh! Right. Is the baby asleep in his cot!

**Lisa**   Is he asleep in his cot!

**Nick**   Right. He asleep in his cot! Sirry iriots.

**Lisa**   Yes. He's fast asleep.

**Nick**   Good.

*Enter* **Brian**.

**Brian**   Here we are then. Come on Richard; all hands to the deck.

**Richard**   Oh, right.

**Lisa**   Ooh. They look nice.

**Brian**   Marks and Sparks.

**Lisa**   Oh, they're very good, Marks and Spencers.

**Brian**   They are.

**Lisa**   They're not cheap.

**Brian**   They're extortionate, but they're very good.

**Nick**   You know a trubber with my wife?

**Brian**   What's that then?

**Nick**   Sometimes she strips and shows her bare behind up in the air.

**Brian**   Oooh. Well.

**Lisa**   It's a joke. He's being funny.

**Brian**   Mmm?

**Nick**   She strips and shows her bare behind up in the air.

**Brian**   Oh, I see.

**Lisa**   See?

**Brian**   I beg your pardon, sir?

**Nick**   She strips.

**Brian**   She strips?

**Nick**   And shows her bare behind . . .

**Brian**   And shows her bare behind . . .

**Nick**   Up in the air.

**Brian**   Up in the air?

**Nick**   At's right, at's what I said.

**Lisa**   That's enough, Nick.

**Nick**   You deaf or sumfink?

**Lisa**   It's funny when Benny does it; when you do it it's just embarrassing.

**Brian**   No, no no. She strips . . . ?

**Nick**   She strips . . . strips . . . over the carpet!

**Brian**   Trips over the carpet!

**Nick**   And so her baby ends up in the air.

**Brian**   She trips and so her baby ends up in the air!

**Nick**   That's right. That's what I said!! Strewth!

*Enter* **Richard** *with food.*

**Brian**   Very good.

**Nick**   Ahhhsoles.

**Brian**   Must have taken you hours.

**Lisa**   Well, little things please little minds.

**Nick**   You have a good screw then?

**Richard**   Sorry?

**Nick**   You have a good screw, then? A good screw! For open a wine!

**Lisa**   Oh. Ha ha ha.

**Richard**   Oh, a corkscrew! Here.

**Nick**   Brimey o rirey!

**Brian**   Oh, I'm going to enjoy myself tonight. But I am very disappointed with your cozzy.

**Richard**   All right, Brian. Just for you.

**Brian**   I knew you'd have something up your sleeve.

**Richard**   Two minutes.

*Exit* **Richard**.

**Brian**   I knew he'd have something up his sleeve. I'll get the rest of the nibbles.

*Exit* **Brian**.

**Lisa**   All right, babe? How was the car today?

**Nick**   Oh, it had a great time. Particularly enjoyed its push-start across the playground by the fourth-form netball team.

**Lisa**   So did you, probably. Max had a nice day. Ate a whole banana. And he said another word, and he's only nine months. He said Dada. It was very clear. Dada. It's a pity you weren't there; I could have pointed at you. That's four words he's got now; Muma, More, Dada, and Yoplait. And his pooh was quite solid today; quite grown up. Of course, on the way to the shops his fan belt broke and I had to call out the RAC, but other than that . . .

*Pause.*

**Nick**   Pardon?

**Lisa**   'Pardon?'

*Enter* **Brian** *with, amongst other things, a large trifle.*

**Brian**   Here we are then; and I'll tell you this for nothing. You don't get one of these out of a packet.

**Lisa**   Ooh lovely, Brian.

**Richard** (*off*)   Brian!

**Brian**   What?

**Richard** (*off*)   Introduce me.

**Brian**   Oh, right. Ladies and gentlemen, here he is, the lad himself . . . Benny Hill.

**Richard** *enters, singing Benny's opening theme. Grey wig, silly grin,* *awful show-biz clothes circa 1972.*

**Brian**   Oh, perfect.

**Lisa**   Oh my God.

**Brian**   That is brilliant.

**Nick**   Very good, mate.

**Richard** (*country bumpkin Benny*)   I said; if you bath in milk use pasteurized, cos pasteurized is best. She said Ernie, I'll be happy if it comes up to me chest!

**Nick**   The wig is brilliant.

**Brian**   Perfect.

**Nick**   Where did you get it?

**Richard**   Oxfam.

**Nick**   Imagine; someone actually wore that. I mean, if that's the sort of hair you haven't got any more it's good riddance, surely?

**Lisa**   Where did you get that jacket?

**Richard**   Well . . .

**Nick**   Institute for the Blind, I should think.

**Lisa**   It's really horrible.

**Richard**   Well, it's um . . .

**Nick**   Gruesome.

**Richard**   It's um . . .

**Brian**   Mine as a matter of fact.

**Richard**   It's Brian's.

**Lisa**   It's a lovely colour.

**Brian**   Oh, it's years old. I thought you were up to something. Who wants another drink?

**Nick** Me.

**Lisa** Me, please.

**Brian** *pours.*

**Nick** Of course, you couldn't actually wear a jacket like that on TV you know; it'd cause linear strobing.

**Brian** I'll have you know I looked very dapper in that, once upon a time.

**Nick** *tastes his wine.*

**Nick** Ah, rubbery.

**Brian** Shouldn't be; do you want another glass?

**Nick** No, it's rubbery. A wine is rubbery!

**Brian** Oh. Sirry iriot. Let's have a sneaky toast before the mob arrive. To Benny.

**Nick** We'll miss you, mate.

**Richard** To Benny.

**Lisa** Rest in peace.

*They sit.*

**Nick** (*quietly, sadly*) Dee dee dee dee dee diddle diddle dee dee diddle diddle dee diddle diddly dum! Dee dee dee . . .

**All** (*joining in separately*) . . . Dee dee diddle diddle dee dee diddle diddle dee diddle diddly dum!

**All** Dee diddle dum diddle dum diddle dum diddle diddle dum dum diddle dum diddle dum diddle diddle dum! Diddle diddle diddle! Diddle diddle dum! Diddle de dum dum!

**Nick** Rom pom tiddle tiddle rom pom oom pom . . .

**All** Rom pom tiddle tiddle rom pom oom pom . . .

**Brian** Pom pom pom pom!

**Lisa**   Rom pom pom pom!

**Richard**   Pom pom pom pom pom!!!

**Eleanor** *enters.*

**All except Eleanor**   Rom pom pom pom pom pom
tiddle pom! Rom pom pom pom pom tiddle tiddle! Tiddle
iddle iddle! Tiddle te tum . . .

*They stop one by one as they notice* **Eleanor**.

**Richard**   Hello Ellie.

**Eleanor**   I thought for a moment I had the wrong house.
But no, right house. Wrong life.

**Brian**   Now put a smile on your face; we're throwing a
party here.

**Eleanor**   I think I'd rather walk into a party thrown
by . . .

**Brian**   Who?

**Eleanor**   No one.

**Richard**   Who?

**Nick**   Who?

**Eleanor**   I was going to say Denis Nillson, but you'd
think I was a horrible person, so I didn't.

**Nick** *laughs a lot. Stops.*

**Nick**   Well, I think it's funny.

**Eleanor**   That's because you are . . .

**Eleanor/Lisa**   . . . a horrible person.

**Richard**   I though you had a class.

**Eleanor**   No one turned up.

**Lisa**   What are you teaching?

**Eleanor**   Classroom skills. No one else here then?

**Brian**   Oh, it's early yet.

**Eleanor**   I need a drink.

**Brian**   Have you got a costume?

**Eleanor**   Have I fuck.

**Nick**   I was hoping you'd come as a Hill's Angel.

**Eleanor**   Dream on.

**Brian**   Stuff a cushion up your cardy and be Bella Emberg.

**Eleanor**   I could finish the gin and come as Bob Todd.

**Richard**   Ellie, it's a party. If you're not going to enjoy yourself, go upstairs and watch television.

**Eleanor**   No.

**Richard**   Have a kip.

**Eleanor**   I'm making an effort!

**Nick**   Richard. (*Sings quietly.*) Will you miss me tonight...

**Brian**   Ohh...

**Lisa**   Oh, yes.

**Richard**   No.

**Nick**   Go on.

**Richard**   Oh, all right.

**Eleanor**   Richard...

**Richard**   Two minutes.

**Richard** *becomes his own approximation of Eric Morecambe.*

**Richard** (*sings*)   Will you miss me tonight. When I'm gone? Will your love be the same...

**Nick** *becomes Ernie Wise.*

**Nick**   What are you doing?

**Richard**  Eh?

**Nick**  What are you doing?

**Richard**  Ah, well I've found something out. I don't need you. You're not a nasset any more, to me. I'm going to do it all by myself. Sing, by myself. I'm going to be a big star.

**Nick**  But you're not doing it right.

**Richard**  Aren't I?

**Nick**  No; you can't be a star on your own.

**Richard**  Oh.

**Nick**  You've got to have backing.

**Richard**  Have you?

**Nick**  Sure. Now I'm a group.

**Richard**  No.

**Nick**  Yeh.

**Richard**  All by yourself?

**Nick**  No, no no no. There's Dick, Sid, and me.

**Richard**  Oh.

**Nick**  Come on, Brian.

**Brian**  Oh, you daft buggers.

**Lisa**  Ellie, you'll love this. We did it at the hospice last Christmas.

**Nick**  Now Dick, he's a boomer.

**Brian**  Boom.

**Richard**  That was good.

**Nick**  And Sid, he an oo-er.

**Richard**  Is he?

**Nick**  Sid; give him an oo-er.

**Lisa**   OooOooOooh.

**Richard**   That's clever that. That's good that.

**Nick**   And me, I'm a ya-ta-ta-ta-er.

**Richard**   Oh, this is great.

**Nick**   We'll make you into a big star.

**Richard**   I'm glad you came.

**Nick**   Right. Here we go fellers . . .

**Lisa**   Left foot, Brian.

**Nick**   A one, two . . .

**Brian**   Boom!

**Lisa**   Oooh!

**Richard**   Ya ta ta ta!

*Repeat.*

**Nick** (*sings*)   Will you miss me tonight, when I'm gone?
Will your love be the same from now on . . .

**Richard**   Ya ta . . . ta . . . ta . . . Ya . . . No, wait, no wait
a minute boys. No, what's happening . . . Hold it lads.
What's happening is I'm ya ta ta ta-ing, you see, I'm ya
ta ta ta-ing instead of Miss-Me-Tonight-ing.

**Nick**   Oh well, perhaps I shouldn't have started it.

**Richard**   Oh.

**Nick**   We'll let Sid start it. Sid, would you like to start it?

**Lisa**   Yes.

**Richard**   Good. That's good.

**Nick**   OK, Sid.

**Lisa**   Left foot, Brian. And one, two . . .

**Brian**   Boom!

**Richard**   Oooh!

**Nick**   Ya ta ta ta!

**Lisa**   Will you miss me tonight, when I'm gone? Will your love be the same from now on . . .

**Richard**   Oooh, no. No, just a . . . hold it boys, you see what's happening . . .

**Brian**   Boom diddy boom diddy boom de boom boom boom . . .

**Richard**   Dick. Dick. Dick. Dick. Dick! He's away, Dick is, isn't he? No you see what's happening is I'm Oooh-ing now. I've ya ta ta ta-ed, I've Oooh-ed . . . I've only got a boom to go.

**Nick**   Perhaps Sid shouldn't have started it.

**Richard**   Well, I didn't want to say anything when you suggested that . . .

**Nick**   Would you like to start it?

**Richard**   Well, if you insist.

**Nick**   Well, all right.

**Richard**   If it'll make it any easier for you. Yes. Well now, this is what happens boys, it's . . . Boom! Oooh! Ya ta ta! Boom! Oooh! Ya ta ta ta! . . .

*Repeat.*

**Others** (*sing*)   Will you miss me tonight, when I'm gone? Will your love be the same from now on . . .

*They applaud themselves.*

**Richard**   It's tough at the top, isn't it?

**Ellie** *remains stony-faced.*

**Brian**   Oh, yes.

**Lisa**   Sid Green and Dick Hills.

**Brian**  The best.

**Richard**  Probably the best sketch ever written.

**Nick**  Oh no.

**Richard**  No?

**Nick**  No I beg to differ. The best sketch ever . . .

**Brian**  With the exception of 'Who's On First Base?'

**Nick**  Yes, right, well, with the exception of 'Who's On First Base?' . . .

**Brian**  Because that's American.

**Richard**  The best British sketch . . .

**Lisa**  Dead Parrot?

**Nick**  No no no no.

**Richard**  What?

**Brian**  Which one?

**Nick** *gets up.*

**Nick**  Hey! Are you putting it around that I'm barmy?

**Brian**  Oh . . . yes!

**Richard**  Good heavens, no.

**Lisa**  Jimmy James.

**Brian**  Oh, brilliant.

**Nick**  Is it him then?

**Richard**  I don't know. Is it you that's putting it around that he's barmy?

**Brian**  I don't want any.

**Richard**  He doesn't want any.

*They laugh.*

**Nick**   Great stuff.

**Lisa**   The one and only.

**Brian**   Jimmy James.

**Eleanor**   I wouldn't be so bewildered by your love for dead comedians if when they were alive you actually laughed at them.

**Brian**   Of course we laugh at them.

**Eleanor**   He doesn't. I've watched him watching them and he doesn't laugh.

**Richard**   Of course I laugh.

**Eleanor**   You might think you do but you don't.

**Richard**   I do.

**Eleanor**   The odd wry smile is not laughter. The occasional meaningful nod is not laughter. A muttered 'very good' or 'oh, excellent', is not laughter. Appreciation it may be and Lord knows you sit there appreciating 'til the cows come home, but laugh you do not!

**Richard**   Ignore her.

**Brian**   What's the time?

**Nick**   It's twenty past . . . ooh, I must get a little hand put on this watch. Eight.

**Brian**   They should have started arriving by now, you know.

**Eleanor**   If they're dressed like you four they've probably all been arrested.

**Nick**   When's Henry coming?

**Brian**   Oh well, he's performing you see. Not until after eleven.

**Nick**   Oh well, they'll be here by then.

**Brian**  Oh yes, they'll all be here by then.

**Lisa**  Actually, I'm not sure they will, not actually.

**Brian**  What do you mean?

**Eleanor**  She's got a massive migraine; there's been a pile-up on the M25 and the Northern line's caught fire.

**Lisa**  Well actually I have got a bit of a headache but that's not it. We had a phone call late this afternoon. From Les Rollins. He said he wasn't going to come.

**Brian**  Oh well, good. I'm glad.

**Lisa**  He said he was having a few people round. He said would we like to come. I said no, of course not; we're having a do at Richard's. Best of British, he said, and put the phone down.

**Brian**  He did what?

**Nick**  Why didn't you tell us?

**Lisa**  I was hoping they might turn up.

**Brian**  A few people round? How many people?

**Lisa**  I don't know.

**Richard**  I shouldn't think many.

**Brian**  I'm the last to wish ill on anyone, but I sometimes wish Les Rollins had died of that heart attack.

**Nick**  No one'll go.

**Richard**  Roger maybe; he and Les seem thick as thieves, but I shouldn't think he'd have the nerve to phone round the entire society. I mean he didn't phone here. I mean, he's not very popular.

**Lisa**  He's been getting more popular.

**Nick**  Rumour has it someone recently touched him with a bargepole.

**Richard**    And it's goodnight from me.

**Nick**    And goodnight from him.

**Brian**    How dare he! How dare he do this!

**Richard**    Calm down, Brian. He may have phoned round, but that doesn't mean anyone's going to choose to go round his place.

**Nick**    Well, not everyone.

**Richard**    Some maybe.

**Nick**    One or two. I bet they bloody will, you know.

**Richard**    Toby wouldn't.

**Nick**    Toby won't.

**Lisa**    He rang to see if you were.

**Brian**    Oh no! It's not on. This society has a constitution. Unwritten maybe, but a constitution all the same.

**Eleanor**    Oh for Christ's sake; it's good riddance to the anoraks, surely? We'll be able to get up and down the hall to the front door without suffocating.

**Nick**    I remember where that second cashcard went now. I gave it to Rollins to pay the printers.

**Brian**    That's embezzlement.

**Richard**    Brian, the night is young. Most of them'll turn up.

**Brian**    If they don't, I'm resigning.

**Eleanor**    If they don't, you won't have to.

**Richard**    Come on, cheer up.

**Brian**    Ooh, I could slap him!

**Richard**    Hey, Nick!

**Richard**    *impersonates Tommy Cooper.*

**Richard**   Bottle, glass. Glass, bottle. Bottle, glass. Heh he he!

*Nick joins in eagerly, does Eric Morcambe's thing with a paper bag. Nick stands behind Richard.*

**Richard**   My name is Harry Worth. I don't know why, but there it is.

*They do the window gag.*

**Richard/Brian/Nick**   Terrrrum tum tum Tum dadada dum!

**Brian**   Maxie!

*Nick goes into Max Miller.*

**Nick** (*Max Miller*)   I've got one for you, lady. But if I crack this joke, don't laugh, 'cos if you laugh the manager'll know it's rude. So, I'm going up this mountain on a very narrow path and suddenly there's this lady in front of me going the other way. She was a nice lady . . . a little bit and some more, a not quite so much, and then a perhaps . . .

*Lisa smiles. Richard and Brian laugh. Eleanor doesn't. Nick ducks out of the door to check the manager isn't listening.*

**Nick**   No, don't! Shh. You'll get me into trouble.

**Richard**   Don't smile; you might crack your face.

**Eleanor**   If I've heard this stuff once . . .

**Nick**   Pay attention. So there she is and there I am and there's a sheer drop one side of me and a vertical cliff the other. I didn't know whether to block her passage or toss myself off. No, shush. Shush. You'll get me arrested. Take a good look lady . . .

**Brian/Nick/Richard**   There'll never be another.

**Richard**   My father used to do Max Miller.

**Brian**   Really?

**Richard**   Once a year, on Boxing Day, between cold turkey for lunch and curried turkey for supper, he'd disappear and come downstairs dressed in some old curtains and he'd launch into Max Miller. Us kids'd be on the carpet; we'd be rolling around. My mother pretending to be shocked. He did a whole routine. Learnt it off a record. It was a big treat for us kids, seeing him muck about like that. Laughing.

**Eleanor**   First time I've ever heard you remember your father fondly.

**Richard**   It's about the only time I can remember him.

**Nick**   I remember him. Scared the life out of me.

**Richard**   Boxing Day's all I remember.

**Eleanor**   He's got a lot to answer for, your father.

**Richard**   I don't think he had any influence on me at all.

**Eleanor**   Ha.

**Richard**   What do you mean 'Ha'?

**Eleanor**   He was a consultant obstetrician. You're a consultant obstetrician. Was that a coincidence?

**Richard**   He'd have been happy whatever I chose.

**Eleanor**   Happy! Your father?

**Richard**   He didn't push me into anything.

**Eleanor**   Some fathers push, some fathers suck. Yours sucked.

**Richard**   Please, Eleanor.

**Eleanor**   He treated your mother like dirt. Virtually ignored her for thirty years then discarded her like a used car, because he fancied a newer model.

**Richard**   How do you know?

**Eleanor**   Because she told me. When we did that big

jigsaw of Mevagissy Harbour together. By the time we'd done the sky, I knew all about your father.

**Richard**   He's got nothing to do with it.

**Eleanor**   We got quite close before she died. She said you were more like him than you ever thought you were.

**Richard**   I'm nothing like him.

**Nick**   There'll never be another!

**Brian**   Oh, there'll never be another! There was of course.

**Nick**   What?

**Brian**   A pretender. Not as good as The Cheeky Chappie, but when it comes to playing an audience, almost as great as Max.

**Nick**   Doddy?

**Brian**   Well yes of course, but no . . . my favourite. My absolute favourite. Richard knows.

**Richard**   Frankie.

**Brian**   Frankie.

**Nick**   Oh well, Frankie!

**Lisa**   Oh yes.

**Nick**   I should say so; yes missus.

**Richard**   No, don't. You mustn't.

**Lisa**   Now apparently, he's a little bit psychic.

**Brian**   Go on Nick.

**Nick**   No, well, what did you expect, class? You've come to the wrong place, then. On what they're paying me you're lucky to get the suit.

**Ellie** *strides across his space to get a cigarette.*

**Nick**   Who rattled your cage? No. Now, before we start this little eisteddfod, I'm going to make a little appeal. It's all right, it's not for money; you've been robbed as it is. No, don't titter. Titter ye not! Well if you must, then for gawdsake all get them out at the same time. Go on missus; get your titters out!

**Brian**   Oh, he's the best.

**Richard**   The best. We went to see Frankie when we were what?

**Nick**   We were nineteen-years-old.

**Richard**   At the Palladium. My father was given tickets by one of the Beverly Sisters who had an ectopic pregnancy, but he couldn't go.

**Nick**   That's what started it for me really, that night.

**Richard**   It was a great night. No don't!

**Nick**   Oh, please yourselves. Best night of my life.

**Lisa**   Oh, thank you very much.

**Brian**   Ooh; hark at her, sat sitting there.

**Nick**   All fur coat and no knickers.

**Lisa**   Charming, I'm sure.

**Nick**   I'm not saying she's a loose woman.

**Brian**   No?

**Nick**   But they'll have to bury her in a Y-shaped coffin.

*Laughter.*

**Brian**   Well, I think it's Ellie's turn.

**Eleanor**   I haven't got a turn.

**Nick**   Come on, Ellie.

**Brian**   Go on Ellie; don't be a partypooper; tell us a joke.

**Richard**   She can't tell jokes.

**Eleanor**   Yes I can.

**Richard**   You don't know any jokes.

**Eleanor**   I know a joke. I overheard a joke in a pub once.

**Richard**   Bet you can't remember it.

**Lisa**   Go on, Ellie.

**Eleanor**   A man took his wife to the doctor. The doctor examined her and told the man she either had Alzheimer's disease or Aids. The man said, which? The doctor said it's impossible to tell. The man said, how can I find out? The doctor said put her in the car, drive her out into the woods about four or five miles, drop her off . . . and if she finds her way back, don't fuck her.

*A pause.* **Nick** *laughs, almost.*

**Eleanor**   If you don't touch me soon. Not sexually, necessarily, not by appointment. But just casually, accidentally even . . . a simple touch. If you can no longer even touch me, I think I shall go mad.

*Long pause.*

**Brian**   You know, I don't dislike this fabric.

**Nick**   No, missus. Don't.

**Lisa**   Excuse me.

**Brian**   What's wrong?

**Lisa**   I'm feeling a bit peculiar.

**Brian**   Oh, sweetheart. Can I help?

**Nick** (*Frankie*)   No, take no notice; she's a peculiar woman.

**Eleanor**   Lisa?

**Nick**   No, don't. Don't encourage her.

**Eleanor**   You've gone very pale.

**Nick**   Poor soul.

**Eleanor**   She looks awful.

**Nick**   No, don't.

**Lisa**   Frankie?

**Nick**   It's cruel.

**Lisa**   Frankie?

**Nick**   Don't mock the afflicted.

**Lisa** *faints.*

**Brian**   Oh dear.

**Eleanor**   Lisa?

**Richard** *becomes a doctor,* **Eleanor** *and* **Brian** *gather round.*

**Eleanor**   Is she all right?

**Richard**   She's just fainted, I think. Has she been ill?

**Nick**   Bit run down.

**Richard**   Lisa?

**Lisa**   Ooh.

**Brian**   Ah.

**Eleanor**   All right, Lisa?

**Brian**   She's all right. She's back.

**Lisa**   Sorry.

**Richard**   Careful. Don't get up.

**Lisa**   Don't want to spoil the party.

**Brian**   You just sit there for a bit.

**Lisa**   Sorry. Ellie. I'm really sorry.

**Eleanor**   What for?

**Lisa**   I am, really.

**Richard**   You should lie down.

**Lisa**   I'm really sorry.

**Richard**   Let's get you upstairs.

**Richard** *carries her out.*

**Brian**   Poor thing.

**Nick**   She'll be all right.

**Eleanor**   Has she seen anyone about those headaches.

**Nick**   Oh yes. She errs on the safe side. Had a load of tests, year before last, all OK. Even had a brain scan. They didn't find anything. Boom boom.

**Brian**   Oh, yes. Ha.

**Eleanor**   Aren't you in the least concerned?

**Nick**   She's highly strung, that's all. Personally I'd string her a bit higher.

**Eleanor**   Nick!

**Nick**   Well, you don't have to live with it. I'm the one it's making ill.

**Richard** *returns.*

**Richard**   She's on our bed.

*Pause.*

**Brian**   What's the time?

**Richard**   It's . . . ooh . . .

**Eleanor**   Please. Don't.

**Richard**   . . . I haven't got a watch on.

**Nick**   It's twenty-five past nine.

**Brian**   They're not coming, are they?

**Eleanor**  That's right Brian; look on the bright side.

*The lights fade.*


**Scene Two**

*The same. Two hours later. They've all been drinking.* **Brian** *is deeply unhappy.* **Eleanor** *brooding.* **Richard** *numb.* **Nick** *merry but quiet.*

**Richard**  What have you achieved? You contributed absolutely nothing to this life. A waste of time you being here at all.

**Brian**  I know.

**Nick**  Shh.

**Richard**  No plaque for you in Westminster Abbey; all you can expect is a few daffodils in a jam jar. A rough hewn stone bearing the words, he came and he went, and in between . . . nothing. Cor, dear oh dear . . .

**Nick**  Hancock.

**Brian**  Hancock.

**Nick**  Ray Galton, Alan Simpson.

**Richard**  No one'll even notice you're not here. After about a year afterwards somebody might say down the pub, 'Where's old Hancock? I haven't seen him around lately.' 'Oh, he's dead you know.' 'Oh, is he?' A right raison d'être that is!

**Nick**  That's right. And they wrote that . . .

**Richard**  That was the last television script they wrote him.

**Nick**  Was it?

**Richard**  The last one.

**Nick**   That's . . . weird.

**Lisa** *enters.*

**Lisa**   Hello.

**Brian**   Oh, there she is.

**Eleanor**   Are you feeling better?

**Lisa**   I fell asleep.

**Eleanor**   How do you feel?

**Lisa**   Oh, much better. Just a bit of a headache.

**Nick**   Les Rollins' flat burned to the ground with no survivors.

**Eleanor**   Leave her alone.

**Brian**   Don't try and cheer me up Nick, I'm not in the mood.

**Lisa**   I'm sorry to be a nuisance. It's the breast feeding, I think. I'm on iron tablets, but apparently they don't dissolve anyway. Oh well. Hello again.

**Brian**   Hello.

**Richard**   Hello.

**Lisa**   No one else came then?

**Eleanor**   Oh yes, they all came. But they were wearing sensible clothes so we didn't let them in.

**Richard**   Look on the bright side Brian. In twenty minutes time you'll have Henry McGee all to yourself.

**Eleanor**   The bright side presumably being the twenty minutes.

**Brian**   I should think Henry's a man of his word.

**Richard**   One of the gentlemen of the profession I should think.

**Brian**  And he'll be more at ease in a small gathering.

**Richard**  That's right.

**Nick**  That's right.

**Brian**  Before he does arrive, there is something I wanted to say. If I don't say it now I never will. So, here goes. This might come as a bit of a shock to you all, coming out of the blue.

**Eleanor**  What's wrong?

**Brian**  Oh, nothing's wrong. I just wanted to say a few words about Benny. Now over the years I've met a number of people who've been acquainted with one or other of the girls that Benny was obliged to work with, and I was always gratified to learn, indeed the girls were often at pains to stress, that at all times he behaved like a perfect gentleman. That for all the necessarily salacious material that they performed with him, there was never, ever, a hint of impropriety. Well, Benny's gone now, and of course the press are going to have a field day. Which is sad because he was always an intensely private man. A solitary, and many believe, celibate man. Well, wherever he is, he'll have to forgive me for this, but I believe otherwise. I believe Benny was gay.

**Nick**  Bloody hell.

**Lisa**  You mean queer?

**Brian**  He was a homosexual, yes. No funny comments please, Ellie.

**Eleanor**  I'm speechless.

**Brian**  Don't mock, because after you've heard what I'm going to say you might wish you hadn't.

**Eleanor**  Sorry, Brian.

**Brian**  Benny was gay. So, I believe, are many other great comedians. Including, and this is not a thing I'd say in public because it's not a thing he's chosen to make public himself, including Frankie Howerd.

**Eleanor**   My world is shattered.

**Ellie** *silenced by a look from* **Brian**.

**Brian**   Frankie is gay. Deep breath. And so am I.

*Pause.*

**Richard**   What?

**Brian**   Gay.

*Long pause.*

**Brian**   There. You see. I knew you'd be speechless.

**Eleanor** *opens her mouth and closes it.*

**Richard**   Well . . .

**Lisa**   Well, well, well.

**Nick** *sniggers. Turns away.*

**Brian**   You're all good friends. Good friends. I hope it won't make any difference.

**Eleanor**   Of course it won't.

**Richard**   Thanks for sharing it with us.

**Brian**   I feel quite light-headed. It's as if a great weight's been lifted off my mind.

**Nick**   Brian . . . ?

**Eleanor**   Nick.

**Brian**   What?

**Nick**   Nothing.

*He turns away again. His shoulders heave.*

**Eleanor**   How long have you known, Brian?

**Brian**   Well to be honest, I've had my suspicions for quite some time. Mum was always on at me to get a girlfriend. Then, I shouldn't tell you this, but I had a little encounter in the post room at work with a dispatch rider and that clinched it really.

**Nick** *snorts.*

You're all a bit shocked, I know. I took a deep breath and told mum. I said Mum, I'm gay. She said Brian, you're not. You're all right. I didn't want to worry her, so I just let it lie.

**Lisa**  You're not really, are you? Queer?

**Eleanor**  Lisa.

**Lisa**  Well, I know he's camp as a row of tents, we've always known that . . .

**Richard**  Lisa . . .

**Lisa**  But I never realized you were actually queer.

**Richard**  I think the word is gay.

**Lisa**  Same difference.

**Nick**  Brian . . .

**Richard**  Well, I think it's great news. I think we should drink on it.

**Eleanor**  Absolutely. To Brian's Coming Out.

**Brian**  Oh. I suppose so. I suppose it is, yes. Out of the closet. I only wish I'd known where I was all these years.

**Eleanor**  To Brian.

**Richard**  To Brian.

**Nick**  To Brian.

**Eleanor**  Our gay friend.

**Brian**  Oh, and look; I'm going to celebrate in style.

*Takes a slip of paper out of his wallet.*

**Eleanor**   What is it?

**Brian**   A ticket to Amsterdam.

**Nick**   Amsterdam?

**Richard**   What are you going to do in Amsterdam?

**Eleanor**   Richard.

**Richard/Nick**   Oh.

**Brian**   I realize some of you . . . that there has to be some adjustment.

**Lisa**   Don't look at me. I'm not homosemitic.

**Nick**   Phobic.

**Lisa**   Phobic. I'm just a bit surprised.

**Nick**   You've known him for years. How could you be surprised?

**Lisa**   Well, we're all surprised aren't we? Aren't we?

**Nick**   I thought you were supposed to be clairvoyant.

**Lisa**   I don't know what you're angry at me for.

**Nick**   You wouldn't know if Christmas was coming.

**Lisa**   Well if he didn't know he was queer, how the bloody hell am I supposed to know; I'm not psychic! Well, I am a little bit, but not like that!

**Nick**   Oh, shut up.

**Lisa**   I'm not Ellie, Nick. Don't tell me to shut up in front of other people.

**Nick**   Then stop talking bollocks.

**Richard**   Steady on, Nick. She's not feeling well.

**Lisa**   Excuse me.

**Lisa** *exits.*

**Eleanor**   What's the matter with you, Nick?

**Nick**   I have to live with her.

**Eleanor**   You chose to live with her.

**Nick**   Whose side are you on?

**Eleanor**   I'm not on anyone's . . . hers!

**Nick**   You take the piss out of everyone all evening and all of a sudden I'm supposed to sit here while she prattles on . . .

**Richard**   Nick. You're out of order, mate.

**Nick**   It's her who's out of order! You don't know the fucking half of it either so mind your own sodding business.

**Brian**   Look, did I start this? I hope I didn't start this.

**Eleanor**   You didn't start anything. Nick, you're pissed.

**Nick**   So would you be.

**Brian**   I need a breath of fresh air.

**Eleanor**   Brian; it's not your fault.

**Brian**   Once round the block. I won't be long.

**Eleanor**   I'll come with you.

**Brian**   No. It is my fault. Bad timing.

*Exit* **Brian**.

**Eleanor**   What is wrong with you two?

**Richard**   I didn't say a word.

**Eleanor**   That was a big step for Brian.

**Nick**   Oh come on Ellie; I've never met a bigger pooftah.

**Eleanor**   It's taken him years to do what he did tonight. It took a lot of courage. More courage than you two could muster put together.

**Richard**   Why am I involved in this all of a sudden?

**Eleanor**   Because you're vile. Both of you. All of you. If it's something you can't snigger at, you run a mile.

**Richard**   What are you talking about?

**Eleanor**   The difference between us.

**Eleanor** *exits, following* **Lisa** *upstairs.*

**Nick**   Sorry.

**Richard**   That's all right mate. I don't know what's going on.

**Nick**   It's been getting worse and worse lately; I'm really tensed up, you know? Getting married was a fucking mistake. You should have talked me out of it when I begged you to.

**Richard**   It's often hard just after your first child; so I've heard.

**Nick**   Yes, well that hasn't helped.

**Richard**   Oh come on Nick; you must be happy about the kid. You always wanted kids.

**Nick**   Are we good friends, Richard?

**Richard**   I hope so.

**Nick**   Because if we're not, I haven't got any.

**Richard**   Yes; we're friends.

**Nick**   I know we go back a long way, but it's not always the same thing, is it? Things change.

**Richard**   If there's something you want to say Nick, say it.

**Nick**   Well yes, there is. Lisa doesn't know this. Couple of years ago I got a bit worried about it all. We'd been trying so long, and she'd started going on about IVF. So I didn't tell her but I went to a clinic in Fulham. Private place, very nice, nice people.

*Pause.*

**Richard**    Mmm.

**Nick**    Long and the short of it is . . . I had some tests
done.

**Richard**    I see.

**Nick**    I'm telling you this in confidence.

**Richard**    Sure.

**Nick**    They actually count the sperm.

**Richard**    Oh, yes.

**Nick**    How many normal, how many swimming. Two
hundred and fifty million sperms per mil of come.

**Richard**    That was your count?

**Nick**    No, that's the average.

**Richard**    I know.

**Nick**    Mine was lower. Mine was nil. Whatsit?

**Richard**    Azoo.

**Nick**    Azoo.

**Richard**    Spermia.

**Nick**    Right. I didn't tell Lisa. Bit of a shock. Three
months later she gave me a bigger one.

**Richard**    Well, there you go. The labs sometimes botch
these things. Put the wrong time on the dish; the slide gets
left on the bench . . .

**Nick**    That's what I thought, so I went to another clinic.
Had it done again.

**Richard**    And?

**Nick**    It's not my kid.

**Richard**   You don't know that.

**Nick**   It's not my kid.

**Richard**   Does Lisa know?

**Nick**   She doesn't know it's not.

**Richard**   You haven't told her?

**Nick**   She hasn't told me. I know she knows it might not be, but she doesn't know I know it's not.

**Richard**   You mean it *might* not be.

**Nick**   The point is she thinks I think it definitely is and I know it definitely isn't.

**Richard**   Why haven't you said anything?

**Nick**   I thought I could cope. I thought I could, but I can't. I hate being with her. I hate her voice. I hate her face. And I hate the kid. What do you think I should do?

*Enter* **Ellie**, *followed by* **Lisa**.

**Eleanor**   Nick. Apologise to your wife.

**Richard**   He's very sorry.

**Eleanor**   Not you. Him.

**Lisa**   Never mind.

**Eleanor**   I mean it. I will not have someone treated like that in my house.

**Richard**   Our house.

**Eleanor**   Don't push your luck. Well?

**Nick**   I'm very sorry.

**Eleanor**   Thank you.

**Nick**   I'm mortally ashamed of myself.

**Lisa**   It's all right.

**Nick**   And I humbly beg . . .

**Eleanor**   Shut up.

*Enter* **Brian**.

**Brian**   Am I still welcome?

**Eleanor**   Oh Brian.

**Richard**   Brian.

**Eleanor**   Come in and sit down.

**Brian**   Only I got as far as the King's Head and I realized, he should be here any minute. Henry.

**Lisa**   Brian. Certain people seem to forget that I was in the business myself for a short time during which I rubbed shoulders with a number of q . . . homosexuals. And quite a few queens. And you can take it from me that not all the queens were homosexuals or all the homosexuals queens. So I never judge from appearances, and Brian, I am certainly not homophobic.

**Eleanor**   Lisa, we know.

**Richard**   We know.

**Lisa**   Good. He is.

**Nick**   No I'm not.

**Lisa**   Yes you are. He is.

**Nick**   Brian . . .

**Lisa**   Don't deny it just for Brian's sake.

**Richard**   Lisa.

**Lisa**   John Inman came on the telly the other night; he turned over and watched a documentary about Haringey Council.

**Nick**   Why do you talk such absolute bollocks?

**Lisa**   Why do you pretend to be everybody's friend when

you're always criticizing them behind their backs?

**Nick**   When did I ever ... ?

**Lisa**   Richard won't lend me his car and Brian's an old queen and Eleanor's a pain in the ...

**Nick**   Lisa! Look, I never ...

**Richard**   Why don't we all just ...

**Lisa**   That's what you said.

**Nick**   Passing comments. Light-hearted banter.

**Lisa**   Vitriol.

**Eleanor**   Listen. If I may be a pain in the arse just for one moment. I wasn't looking forward to this evening. I've got problems of my own. Well, of Richard's. Well, Richard, basically.

**Richard**   Don't call me Richard.

**Eleanor**   Sorry Trevor.

**Nick**   Trevor?

**Eleanor**   I'm not preserving this thin veneer of civilized behaviour over the barren God-awful mess that is my marriage so that you lot can act like the Borgias, so cheer up or go home!

**Lisa**   Sorry.

**Brian**   We couldn't go yet Ellie. Henry'll be here any minute.

**Eleanor**   You see? There is always something to look forward to.

*Telephone rings.*

**Eleanor**   Would you mind answering that, Philip?

**Lisa**   Philip?

**Nick**   Who's Trevor?

**Richard**  Seven three eight four. Hello Toby. Are you? Good. No, we're having a great time here too. Has he? I see. Yes, we were wondering. Did he? Has he? Yeh. I don't think I can Toby, not really. Well, actually Toby, it's a loyalty thing. Well, I don't suppose you would.

*Puts phone down.*

**Brian**  He's gone there, hasn't he?

**Richard**  Rollins told Henry McGee there'd been a change of venue. Turned up with Ray Cooney apparently. And June Whitfield.

**Brian**  Well, that's it then; I resign.

**Nick**  He asked you over, did he?

**Richard**  Oh well, we're all welcome to go over.

*Pause.*

**Brian**  Well I'm not.

**Nick**  Oh, I'm not.

**Richard**  I said I wasn't.

**Lisa**  When you meet a famous person, it's never as exciting as you'd think. They just look the same but smaller. I bet they're all dead small.

**Nick**  It doesn't matter what bloody size they are, does it?

**Lisa**  You know what my mother once said to Jimmy Clitheroe? She was in Dick Whittington with Jimmy Clitheroe, this is true, and he came up to her and he said 'What would you say to a little fuck?' and she said . . .

**All**  'Piss off, little fuck'.

**Lisa**  I told you that then?

**Nick**  She made it up.

**Lisa**  It's true.

**Nick**   She more likely said, 'Yes, please.'

**Lisa**   She's six-foot, my mum.

**Nick**   Probably explains why you're four-foot ten.

**Lisa**   Don't start.

**Nick**   Well I've heard stranger theories about your genetic history.

**Lisa**   Nick, please.

**Nick**   I mean you've said it yourself; your mother wasn't exactly choosy, was she?

**Lisa**   I never said that.

**Eleanor**   Leave her alone.

**Nick**   Tell them your theory.

**Lisa**   I haven't got a theory.

**Nick**   Go on, tell them your theory.

**Eleanor**   Nick!

**Nick**   You may not realize it but we are looking at the illegitimate daughter of . . .

**Lisa**   Nick! There are certain things shared between a man and wife that are personal things. Things other people wouldn't be interested in anyway.

**Richard**   Right.

**Brian**   Absolutely.

**Lisa**   All right?

**Nick**   Right.

*Pause.*

**Richard**   Of who?

**Nick**   Sid James.

**Richard/Brian**  Sid James!

**Lisa**  I only said it once! It was just a thought! It was only something I thought once!

**Nick**  Different woman every film apparently. Lunchtimes, in his caravan.

**Richard**  Of course; *Carry On Matron*.

**Brian**  Seriously?

**Lisa**  There were a couple of photos, that's all, and Nick said . . .

**Nick**  You said . . .

**Lisa**  I didn't say it. I said she used to speak very fondly of him. You're the one who got out Halliwell's Film Guide and worked out the dates.

**Nick**  Dates work out perfectly.

**Lisa**  I never said . . .

**Nick**  I mean there is a resemblance, you have to admit it.

**Lisa**  Nick! It's not true.

*Pause.*

**Lisa**  It's not true.

**Nick** (*Sid's laugh*)  Yuk yuk yuk yuk yuk.

**Lisa**  Shut up!

**Brian**  Even if it was true . . .

**Eleanor**  Brian.

**Richard**  Nothing to be ashamed of, quite the contrary.

**Lisa**  Please, Richard.

**Richard**  No, I mean seriously; what's on your birth certificate?

**Eleanor**  Richard! Mind your own business.

**Richard**  Well he was a notorious womanizer. Propositioned every woman he met.

**Eleanor**  How would you know?

**Nick**  Takes one to know one, eh mate?

**Eleanor**  Well he wouldn't know one; he's been celibate for a year and a half.

**Lisa**  Hu!

**Richard**  Could we keep our private lives private?

**Eleanor**  Pardon?

**Richard**  Could we just wait . . .

**Eleanor**  Not you; her.

**Richard**  All I said was . . .

**Eleanor**  I heard what you said; what did she say?

**Lisa**  I didn't say anything

**Eleanor**  You said 'Hu!'

**Lisa**  No I didn't.

**Eleanor**  Yes you did. You said 'Hu!'

**Lisa**  No, I didn't say 'Hu!', I said 'Ahah!'

**Eleanor**  So I say Richard's celibate and you say 'Ahah!'?

**Lisa**  Mmm?

**Eleanor**  So what does that mean? 'Ahah!'

**Lisa**  Well, it explains why you two aren't getting on so I said 'Ahah!' meaning now we know why Ellie's in such a foul . . . well, why she's acting a bit . . . well, why she's, I mean why you . . . aren't very happy at the moment.

**Eleanor**  But you didn't say 'Ahah!', you said 'Hu!'

**Lisa**  Well, I meant 'Ahah!'

**Eleanor** (*to* **Richard**)  Are you screwing someone else?

*Pause.*

**Brian**  Well, I think it's time for Uncle Brian to wend his weary way . . .

**Richard**  Are you off, Bri?

**Eleanor**  Sit down, Brian. Are you screwing someone else?

**Richard**  Could we talk about this later?

**Eleanor**  Oh, I should think so. We'll talk about it later just as soon as we've finished talking about it right now. Lisa.

**Lisa**  Mmmm?

**Eleanor**  Has my husband told you he's screwing someone else?

**Lisa**  Oh. Well . . . I don't want to get involved in this.

**Eleanor**  You said 'Hu!' Which means he's told you something I don't know. Which means that you must know him a damn bloody sight more . . .

*Long pause.* **Brian** *stands.*

Sit down, Brian. If at this late stage in your life you intend to enter the sexual arena, I think you'd better stay and watch this.

**Lisa**  Take me home, please? Nick?

**Eleanor**  Don't think about standing up Lisa, because you'd never make it to the door.

**Richard**  Ellie.

**Eleanor**  You sat with me on those horrible chairs in Miriam's room and you said you didn't want to be touched. You said it was nothing to do with me. You said

you felt No Desire. You sounded like Christ on the cross.
So in spite of my desperation I have been patient, in spite
of my bewilderment I have been understanding, in spite of
my feeling of utter abandonment ... I've been hanging on
in there. Trying to help you come through this terrible
thing. And all this time ... How often? Don't tell me; I
don't care. All this time you've been screwing the
illegitimate daughter of Sid James. I'm beginning to see the
resemblance.

**Richard**   I think we should let these people go home.

**Lisa**   I really have got a really bad headache now.

**Eleanor**   Maybe someone's going to die.

**Lisa**   I think it's a migraine.

**Eleanor**   Probably you, then.

**Lisa**   Look, it's not true! You've got hold of completely
the wrong end of the stick. It's not true, is it Richard?

*Long pause.*

You sod. Ellie, it wasn't an affair or anything. It was
completely meaningless.

**Eleanor** *strides towards* **Lisa**. **Nick** *catches her arm.*

**Nick**   Ellie. No. Don't. Leave her alone.

**Nick** *rises and goes to* **Lisa**.

**Lisa**   It was his idea, I didn't even fancy him. He said
you only live once. He said he'd never wanted anyone like
he wanted me. He said I was ...

**Nick**   What?

**Lisa**   Beautiful.

**Nick** *sticks one of the custard pies in her face.*

**Eleanor**   Now *that's* funny.

**Brian**   Oh dear, oh dear.

**Richard**  Steady on, mate . . .

**Nick**  What!?

**Richard**  Nick . . .

**Nick**  What?! I'm sorry, did you speak? You got something to say to me?

**Richard**  Nick, it was nothing.

**Lisa**  It was nothing to do with you, Ellie.

**Eleanor**  Nothing to what?

**Nick** *throws food at* **Richard**.

**Nick**  You disloyal, lying, two-faced fucking shit-head.

**Richard**  For Christ's sake mate.

**Nick**  Don't mate me, you toad. You fucking parasite.

**Eleanor**  Mind the furniture, Nick.

**Lisa**  It was purely physical, Ellie. Completely mindless.

**Eleanor**  Well, in your case it would have to be.

**Lisa**  Men need a certain amount of sex Ellie; if they can't get it at home . . .

**Eleanor** *goes for* **Lisa**.

**Eleanor**  You witless little tart!

**Brian**  No!

**Brian** *tries to stop* **Eleanor**. *He grabs her skirt, accidentally ripping it off. Reveals bimbo underwear beneath.* **Eleanor** *hurls forwards, slaps* **Lisa**, *then hides herself, embarrassed.* **Brian** *hurls backwards, knocking* **Richard** *over just as* **Nick** *hurls a pie.* **Brian** *gets the pie.* **Nick** *throws another,* **Richard** *ducks, and* **Lisa** *gets the pie.* **Richard** *attempts to defend himself with a soda siphon; squirts himself, then* **Nick**. **Nick** *looks for something to retaliate with.*

**Nick**  Eighteen years I've known you. Eighteen sodding years!

**Nick** *breaks a bottle.*

**Richard**   No!

**Brian**   Oh, no.

**Eleanor**   Nick. No.

**Nick**   I'll cut your fucking heart out.

**Eleanor**   Nick. No.

**Eleanor** *takes it from him.*

**Nick**   Careful.

**Eleanor**   I've got it.

**Nick**   Don't cut yourself.

**Eleanor**   I'm fine.

**Nick**   I'm sorry.

**Eleanor**   It's all right. Sit down now. Calm down. Richard, sit down. Nick's all right. He's not going to hurt anyone.

**Richard** *sits.*

**Eleanor**   Are you all right?

**Lisa**   Loose tooth.

**Eleanor**   Leave it alone. The gum'll harden up.

**Eleanor** *hands* **Lisa** *some whisky.*

**Lisa**   K'you.

**Brian**   That's better. Lets try and keep a sense of proportion.

**Eleanor**   Brian's right. It's important to keep things in perspective.

**Brian**   Act with a bit of dignity.

**Eleanor**   That's the word I was looking for.

*She empties the trifle over* **Richard**.

**Richard**    What the hell are you wearing, anyway?

**Eleanor**    What, this? My little tribute to Benny. I was saving it for later. It was going to be just for you, but what the hell. What is it about her then? What's she got that I haven't? That can't be it, surely? Big tits? Blonde hair? Short fat hairy legs? It's not sex then? It's not all bodies you find repellent? Just mine? These particular breasts, these particular legs, this particular cunt?

**Richard**    Don't, Ellie.

**Eleanor**    Well then what?

**Richard**    She's different, that's all.

**Eleanor**    Oh I see. Different.

**Lisa**    Ellie; you'll catch cold.

**Eleanor**    Shut up, Sidney.

**Richard**    Please, Ellie.

**Eleanor**    Look at this though; whoever this is. I would have been this for you.

*She sits.* **Brian** *tears up his ticket to Amsterdam. The phone rings.*

**Richard**    Yes? What? (*Pause.*) Yes. Thanks, Toby. Bye.

*Puts phone down.*

**Brian**    What now?

**Richard**    He's dead, Brian.

**Brian**    Les Rollins?

**Richard**    No.

**Brian**    Who then?

**Richard**    Frankie Howerd.

**Brian**    When?

**Richard**    Tonight. They just found him.

*Baby cries. After a while,* **Lisa** *rises.*

**Lisa**    It was his heart.

*Exit* **Lisa**.

**Eleanor**    Never rains but it pours, does it? Nick? Want to come upstairs with me and be different? Anyone here want to fuck me then, or shall I put my clothes back on? Richard. I want you and your bones out of here tonight.

**Richard**    We'll discuss it later.

**Eleanor**    We will not discuss it. If you want to leave, you will leave tonight.

**Richard**    If that's what you want.

**Eleanor**    It's not what I want.

**Lisa** *returns with the baby.*

**Lisa**    Nick. Do you want to drive us home, or shall I?

**Nick**    I'll drive.

**Richard**    I don't think you should Nick; you're not sober.

**Nick**    I'm fine.

**Richard**    No, Nick. You can't drive.

**Nick**    What fucking business is it of yours?

**Eleanor**    Maybe he's right, Nick.

**Nick**    I'm perfectly capable of driving *my* wife, and *my* child, safely home.

**Lisa**    I'll drive. I haven't drunk much. It was just a silly thing. Ellie? Nick, it was just ... Tell them.

**Richard**    It was nothing.

**Lisa**    And it was only ... twice.

**Richard**    Once.

**Lisa**   Once.

**Richard**   Twice. Once or twice.

**Lisa**   And we were very careful. Weren't we? Tell him.

**Richard**   We were careful.

**Nick**   I don't want to know.

**Lisa**   I want you to know. I want you to know the baby . . .

**Nick**   Lisa! If it's finished, it's finished.

**Lisa**   It is finished.

**Richard**   It's finished.

**Nick**   Then it's done with.

**Lisa**   I just wanted you to know.

**Nick**   I'll start her up.

**Richard**   Need a push?

**Nick**   If she needs a push I'll push her.

*Exit* **Nick**.

**Lisa**   I've left his things upstairs.

**Richard**   I'll get them.

*Exit* **Richard**.

**Lisa**   Ellie . . .

**Eleanor**   Who do you love?

**Lisa**   What?

**Eleanor**   It's a simple question. Who do you love?

**Lisa**   Um . . . well . . .

**Eleanor**   Do you love anyone?

**Lisa**   Well Graham Fisher, if you must know.

**Eleanor**   Who's he?

**Lisa**   Man I met at work.

**Eleanor**   You're screwing a man you met at work as well?

**Lisa**   Ellie! What sort of a woman do you think I am? What Graham and I share is beyond sex. Sex with Graham would be too real. You wouldn't understand.

*Enter* **Richard**.

**Richard**   Here.

**Lisa**   Thank you.

*Enter* **Nick**.

**Nick**   Ready?

**Lisa**   Yes.

**Nick**   Put him in the car.

**Lisa**   Come on then.

**Nick**   I'll follow you.

**Lisa**   Nick?

**Nick**   Put him in the car.

*Exit* **Lisa**. **Nick** *goes to* **Richard** *and stands facing him. He clenches, unclenches his fists, then clamps* **Richard**'s *head between spread hands. Almost as if he's going to kiss him. Bursts into tears. Embraces* **Richard**, *then lets him go and takes time to recover.*

**Nick**   Stay away from us.

*Exit* **Nick**.

**Richard**   Can we talk in the morning?

**Eleanor**   It's not his is it?

**Richard**   I don't know.

**Eleanor**   He knows.

**Richard**  Ellie, it meant nothing.

**Eleanor**  Nothing doesn't cry for its mother.

**Richard**  I'm going to have a shower.

**Eleanor**  I meant what I said.

**Richard**  I'll sleep on the sofa.

**Eleanor**  You'll sleep with me. Or you'll leave. Tonight.

**Richard**  This is my home.

**Eleanor**  Don't do this. Don't make it me. Don't make me make you do what you damn well know you want to.

*Tries to take off her wedding ring.*

**Richard**  Where shall I go?

**Eleanor**  You can stay at Brian's. Can he stay at yours?

**Brian**  Oh, yes. He can stay at mine.

*Exit* **Richard**. **Eleanor** *tries to take off her ring. Looks at* **Brian***'s Amsterdam ticket.*

**Eleanor**  Do you want some sellotape for this?

**Brian**  Oh, I'm not bothered. I don't think I could cope. I've got my little flat. I've got some good friends. And I enjoy a good laugh now and again; why spoil it? Things rarely turn out the way you expect, do they? And you sit there thinking, I should have seen this coming. And then you realize I did, I did see this coming. And I sent out invitations.

**Eleanor**  My last ten years with him. He'll end up with some twenty-four-year-old, when he's ready. They'll have a cottage full of kids. And I'll have a couple of cats, a stall on Camden market and the odd holiday in Florence.

**Brian**  Sounds utter bliss.

**Eleanor**  I'll hang myself first. All the little taps inside me are turning themselves off.

**Brian**   You don't really want him to go, do you?

*She looks up. Enter* **Richard** *with bag, a few things stuffed in.*

**Richard**   I'm not sure this is the way we should do this.

**Eleanor**   What is the way we should do this?

**Richard**   There are better ways.

**Eleanor**   I don't think so.

**Brian**   We off then?

**Richard**   Looks like it.

**Brian** *rises, gives* **Richard** *a key.* **Eleanor** *tries to get her wedding ring off.*

**Brian**   Let yourself in. I'll come across when I've done some tidying up.

**Eleanor**   That's all right, I'll do that.

**Brian**   It won't take five minutes.

*Exit* **Brian**.

**Richard**   Ellie.

**Eleanor**   Go away.

**Richard**   Listen.

**Eleanor**   Don't touch me. Please don't.

**Richard**   Are you sure this is what you want?

**Eleanor**   You know what I want.

**Richard**   You want me to go?

**Eleanor**   I want a baby! I want a baby! I want a baby!

**Eleanor** *breaks down. Hurts her hand trying to get her ring off.*

**Eleanor**   All right. Stay. Stay, all right?

**Richard**   Well ... I've packed now. I may as well ...

**Eleanor**    What?

**Richard**    Go.

**Eleanor**    I see.

**Richard**    Bye.

*Exit* **Richard**. *The ring comes off quite easily.*

**Brian**    I've put the kettle on.

**Eleanor**    You don't have to stay; I'll be all right.

**Brian**    Oh, I'd rather. Shouldn't be you sitting on your own.

**Eleanor**    I'd better start practicing.

**Brian**    Look, if you want me to go I'll go. Now do you want me to go?

**Eleanor**    No.

**Brian**    I'll stay then.

**Eleanor**    Thank you.

*He sits. They hold hands.*

**Brian**    You smell nice.

**Eleanor**    Four Seven Eleven.

**Brian**    Oh, that's nice. She'd have liked that.

**Eleanor**    Poor old Frankie.

**Brian**    No, I didn't expect that. All of a sudden everyone's dying. And you never expect it. I watched mum die for two years, but I never expected it. Oh. I miss her so much.

**Eleanor**    Oh, Brian.

**Brian**    What we both need is a nice young man.

**Eleanor**    A nice virile young man.

**Brian**   A nice virile young man who's looking for love.

**Eleanor**   Or in my case, for his mother.

**Brian**   Could be the same chap then.

**Eleanor**   You can have him after me.

**Brian**   I wouldn't deprive you.

**Eleanor**   I wouldn't want him for long. I babysat for them last week. He wouldn't go to sleep. I did something I was so ashamed of, but I couldn't not. I crept upstairs, took off my top, and let him suck. I can still feel his mouth.

*She closes her eyes.* **Brian** *smells her, then touches her breast.*

**Eleanor**   Brian.

**Brian**   Mmm?

**Eleanor**   What are you doing?

**Brian**   You're a very attractive woman, Ellie.

**Eleanor**   You're a homosexual, Brian.

**Brian**   I know.

**Eleanor**   But thanks.

**Brian**   Mum used to say I was always one to show willing.

**Brian** *begins to sing quietly: Frankie Howerd's 'Three Little Fishies'\*.*

**Eleanor** *joins in. They sing until they're laughing too much to continue.*

**Brian**   Well, you've got to see the funny side, haven't you?

*Fade.*

---

\* *Three Little Fishies* by Saxie Dowell. ©Campbell Connelly & Co. Ltd.

## Methuen Contemporary Dramatists
### *include*

Peter Barnes (three volumes)
Sebastian Barry
Edward Bond (six volumes)
Howard Brenton
  (two volumes)
Richard Cameron
Jim Cartwright
Caryl Churchill (two volumes)
Sarah Daniels (two volumes)
David Edgar (three volumes)
Dario Fo (two volumes)
Michael Frayn (two volumes)
Peter Handke
Jonathan Harvey
Declan Hughes
Terry Johnson
Bernard-Marie Koltès
Doug Lucie
David Mamet (three volumes)

Anthony Minghella
  (two volumes)
Tom Murphy  (four volumes)
Phyllis Nagy
Peter Nichols (two volumes)
Philip Osment
Louise Page
Stephen Poliakoff
  (three volumes)
Christina Reid
Philip Ridley
Willy Russell
Ntozake Shange
Sam Shepard (two volumes)
David Storey (three volumes)
Sue Townsend
Michel Vinaver (two volumes)
Michael Wilcox

# Methuen World Classics
*include*

Jean Anouilh (two volumes)
John Arden (two volumes)
Arden & D'Arcy
Brendan Behan
Aphra Behn
Bertolt Brecht (six volumes)
Büchner
Bulgakov
Calderón
Anton Chekhov
Noël Coward (five volumes)
Eduardo De Filippo
Max Frisch
Gorky
Harley Granville Barker
  (two volumes)
Henrik Ibsen (six volumes)
Lorca (three volumes)
Marivaux

Mustapha Matura
David Mercer (two volumes)
Arthur Miller (five volumes)
Molière
Musset
Clifford Odets
Joe Orton
A. W. Pinero
Luigi Pirandello
Terence Rattigan
W. Somerset Maugham
  (two volumes)
Wole Soyinka
August Strindberg
  (three volumes)
J. M. Synge
Ramón del Valle-Inclán
Frank Wedekind
Oscar Wilde

Printed in the United Kingdom
by Lightning Source UK Ltd.
128438UK00001B/12/A